HUDSON TAYLOR'S LEGACY

A SERIES OF MEDITATIONS

HUDSON TAYLOR'S LEGACY

A SERIES OF MEDITATIONS

Christian Focus

© Christian Focus Publications
ISBN 1 85792 492 4

Published in 1999
by
Christian Focus Publications,
Geanies House, Fearn, Ross-shire,
Scotland, IV20 1TW, Great Britain.

Cover design by Owen Daily

TO
THE FOLLOWERS
OF THEM
WHO THROUGH FAITH AND PATIENCE
INHERIT THE PROMISES

Contents

Part 2: The Legacy of His Life

Part 3: The Legacy of His Work

Part 4: The Ever-present Leader

JAMES HUDSON TAYLOR

Born at Barnsley, Yorks, May 21, 1832
Sailed for China, September 19, 1853
Surrendered to God as Leader of C.I.M, June 25, 1865
Died at Changsha, China, June, 1905

Remember them that were your leaders,
Who spoke to you the Word of God;
Look upon the end of their life,
And follow the example of their faith.

JESUS CHRIST
is the same
Yesterday and Today and for Ever.

Be not carried away with manifold and strange doctrines;
For it is good that the heart be established by Grace.

(Hebrews 13:7, 8, 9).
Conybeare & Howson's translation.

FOREWORD

John Bunyan, in his Dedication of *Grace Abounding*, wrote: 'I have sent you here enclosed, a drop of that honey that I have taken out of the carcase of a lion. I have eaten myself thereof, and am much refreshed thereby. Temptations, when we meet them at first, are as the lion that roared upon Samson; but if we overcome them, the next time we see them, we shall find a nest of honey within them. The Philistines understood me not'.

In this little book we have sought to conserve and to present to the reader some of the distilled spiritual experiences and counsels of Hudson Taylor.

For many years we have had frequent occasion to delve among the early records of the China Inland Mission and to feel their tonic influence. More recently, when writing *Hudson Taylor: the Man who believed God*, we felt again the value of Hudson Taylor's devotional articles, articles written out of his own costly and inwrought experience. These bear all the stamp of life, and reveal, not in theory but in practice, the principles upon which he founded his work. As it seemed unpardonable to leave these treasures permanently buried in publications long out of print, the Centenary of Hudson Taylor's birth appeared a fitting opportunity to republish a selection in a more permanent guise. And amongst these we have included fifteen meditations, culled from some unpublished personal letters.

At the same time, it has been thought better to break these articles up into short daily meditations, rather than reprint them *en masse* and unrelated to the occasions which called them forth. We believe the course adopted, though it has had its difficulties and its losses, will justify itself. Great traditions and great truths are not inherited automatically. The rich experiences of another cannot be early transferred or appropriated; they must be learned in life's school. For this reason, we believe, a series of short readings suitable for daily meditation over a somewhat prolonged period will be more helpful than a book which can be skimmed in a few hours.

In condensing and standardizing to one-page-length one hundred and twenty readings, some sacrifice has been inevitable; yet what is printed is, apart from the necessary abbreviations, substantially as originally written. It may perhaps be mentioned that the severe limitations of space have excluded references to chapter and verse, and to the versions quoted.

There is a word towards the close of the Book of *Ecclesiastes* which has somewhat perplexed the translators, and in concluding this Foreword we venture to refer to two possible renderings. Following Delitzsch and others, the Variorum Teacher's Bible renders the verse as follows: 'The words of the wise are as goads, and the sayings fitly joined together are as nails fastened in; they be given from one Shepherd.' As editor our desire and aim has been that these collected sayings of Hudson Taylor might be fitly framed together. The 'apples of gold' are presented as his, but we must accept responsibility for the casket or frame in which they are set.

But there is another rendering of Ecclesiastes 12:11 which has fascinated us. This reads: 'A wise man's words are as goads, and his collected sayings are like nails driven home; they put the mind of one man into many a life.' As a 'collector of sentences' – see the R.V. margin – we shall feel that our labour has been more than worth while if this little book of meditations helps to put the mind of Hudson Taylor into many a life.

Marshall Broomhall
19 September, 1931

WHY COMMEMORATE?

There is a command in the first Church Manual, hardly later than the age of the Apostles, which charges the Christian 'to remember day and night the teachers that speak to him the Word of God' – Westcott.

Why Commemorate?

Remember them that were your leaders (Hebrews 13:7).

'There is one thought that dejects me,' wrote Sir Thomas Browne in *Religio Medici*; it is 'that my acquired parts must perish with myself, nor can be legacied to my honoured friends'. That was written in the 1600s. Today his writings have become a classic, and his name a fragrant memory. Like Milton he had left something that posterity would 'not willingly let die'. Clearly it is not only what men leave that matters, but what others conserve of their spiritual patrimony. Many a priceless inheritance has been lost or squandered, through neglect and forgetfulness. We still need to pray:

Lord God of Hosts, be with us yet,
Lest we forget – lest we forget.

More than one of David's Psalms were written specifically 'to bring to remembrance'. In the forward rush of life today we are in no small danger of failing to cultivate memory. And yet, of all God's good gifts, few, if any, excel this wondrous faculty. Without it life would be a blank. With it we possess all things. The foxes have holes and the birds of the air have nests, but even they without memory could not find them. Man's plight would be far worse. Without memory he would soon perish from the earth. With it he may become the heir of the ages, enriched beyond all measure. Yet how little we think about this great endowment!

There are few nobler passages in St. Augustine's *Confessions* than those in which he pours out his heart before God concerning 'the fields and spacious palaces of memory'. Figure is piled upon figure as he dilates on this wondrous faculty. It is a 'vast court' where all heaven, earth and sea assemble; a 'great harbour' where life's rich argosies store their treasures; 'a great

17

receptacle' stored with the images of things great and many; 'a boundless chamber' of which no man hath ever sounded the bottom. Men go abroad, he says, to admire the mountains, the seas, and the circuit of the stars, and yet they pass themselves by. 'A wonderful admiration surprises me, amazement seizes me,' he cried as he explores this mysterious and measureless capacity. 'Great is the power of memory, a fearful thing.' He finds it even the home of God Himself. 'What manner of lodging hast Thou framed in me? What manner of Sanctuary hast Thou builded in me? Thou hast given this honour to my memory, to reside in it.' This is not hyperbole, or an indulgence in rhetoric, for was it not the enshrinement in the heart and memory of His disciples that Christ coveted when He said: 'This do in remembrance of Me?'

It is no wonder that the Scriptures have given high place to this amazing faculty, for out of it are the issues of life. With it we may enrich or ruin character. Every moment is freighted with some influence from the past to bless or blight the soul. We cannot therefore afford to dispense with the inspiration which comes from the contemplation of those in whom God's power and grace have been made visible. This is no small part of our spiritual heritage. And so the writer of the Epistle to the Hebrews, in his closing appeals, says: 'Remember your former leaders, men that spake unto you the Word of God, and considering the issue of their manner of life, imitate their faith.'

The late Bishop Handley Moule, in one of his devotional commentaries, has a characteristically beautiful exposition of this verse. We cannot do better than quote it, for it will answer our question: Why commemorate?

'Twice over,' he writes, 'the pastors of the Church are mentioned here (verses 7, 17); but how? As "leaders", "guides", ἡγούμενοι: as those who "speak the word of God", as those whose vigilance over the souls of the flock claims a loving and grateful loyalty.' After speaking of the early verses of the chapter he writes:

18

'Then comes the passage where the departed "guides" are commemorated. Whoever they were, were they a Stephen and a James, or saints utterly unknown to us, that passage is precious in its principles, true for all time, of remembrance and appeal. It consecrates the fidelity of the Christian memory. It assures us that to cherish the names, the words, the conduct, the holy lives, the blessed deaths, of our teachers of days long done is no mere indulgence of unfruitful sentiment. It is natural to the Gospel, which, just because it is the message of an unspeakably happy future, also sanctifies the past which is the living antecedent to it. Just because we look with the love of hope toward "our gathering together unto Him", we are to turn with the love of memory toward all the gifts of God given to us through the holy ones with whom we look to be "gathered together". "The exit of their walk of life" is to be our study, our meditation. We are to "look it up and down" ($\dot\alpha\nu\alpha\theta\epsilon\omega\rho\upsilon\nu\tau\epsilon\varsigma$) as we would some great monument of victory, and from that contemplation we are to go back into life, "to imitate their faith", to do just what they did, treating the unseen as visible, the hoped-for as present and within our embrace. Thank God for this authorization and hallowing of our recollections. Precious indeed is its assurance that the sweetness of them (for all its ineffable element of sadness, as eyes and ears are hungry for the faces and the voices gone, for the look and tone of the preacher, the teacher, through whom we first knew the Lord, or knew Him better) is no half-forbidden luxury of the soul, but a means of victorious grace.'

Believing then that remembrance is no idle indulgence, but rather an essential to vigorous life, 'a means of victorious grace', we welcome this opportunity to give it scope.

'Time is the great enemy', a well-known philosopher has said. From its merciless encroachments nothing seems exempt. How ruthless it can be! Before its sway mighty kingdoms are brought low, and marble monuments crumble into dust. But memory can stand against its power and perpetuate the past. While the earliest and original manuscripts recording the words of Christ have passed away, yet the memory of His disciples has, all down the ages, kept unbroken the ordinance instituted with the words, 'Do this in remembrance of Me'. That Feast of Holy Memory has outlived the oldest of our written records, being 'written not with ink, but with the Spirit of the living God; not in tables of stone, but in tables that are hearts of flesh.'

'Some sleep,' says Bunyan, 'when they should keep awake, and some forget when they should remember, and this is why some pilgrims come off losers. Pilgrims should watch, and remember,' he adds, 'for from want of doing so, ofttimes their rejoicing ends in tears and their sunshine in a cloud.' Which piquant counsel is only another way of saying: 'Remember them that were your leaders, and imitate their faith.' This then we take to be sufficient justification for this little book.

PART 1

THE LEGACY OF
HIS MESSAGE

The noblest truths are not given us for an intellectual luxury, still less for a moral opiate or a spiritual charm. They are for the inspiration of our whole being, for the hallowing and for the bracing of every power outward and inward with which we are endowed, for use in the busy fields of common duty – Westcott.

The Legacy of His Message

Remember them ... which spake unto you the Word of God
(Hebrews 13:7).

A man with a message, especially a message from God, is a man to remember. He is made memorable by his commission. Such a man would not easily be forgotten by those who heard God's Good News for the first time, as was probably the case with the Hebrews addressed. Yet, such forgetfulness was evidently possible; hence the exhortation. Those to whom that message is not new are not only in danger of forgetting their obligations, but even of being unconscious of them.

The man who can command attention and arouse the imagination concerning the familiar truths, who can make us see in the old what we never saw before is no less to be remembered. His task may be the harder of the two. The peril of the proverbial is so great that Stevenson prayed that God would 'stab' his 'spirit broad awake', if God's message knocked upon his sullen heart in vain.

'Thou seest many things,' cried Isaiah, 'but thou observest not.' That is the curse of today. We live in a world largely inattentive to and insensible of the eternal because of the multitude of clamant and aggressive earthly voices.

So many cries are uttered now-a-days,
That scarce a song, however clear and true,
Will thread the justling tumult safe, and reach
The ear of men buz-filled with poor denays.

One of Hudson Taylor's outstanding gifts was his power to give point to a message already blunted by constant repetition. Old truths which had become commonplace, responsibilities which were admitted but seldom shouldered, facts which were acknowledged but largely ignored, became in his hands an irresistible challenge.

23

'May God take these, His precious truths,' he cried 'and write them upon our hearts; making them, not matters of mere creed or head-knowledge, but part and parcel of our spiritual and mental being.' A merely notional assent to him was deadly; it must be a living conviction. 'Oh, the need of reality in this world of shams!' he wrote. 'Base coin is so abundant that the world is beginning to question the existence of the true gold from the royal mint. The world needs that the witness of true discipleship be given to Christ in our critical, sceptical age perhaps more than ever.'

Hudson Taylor lives in the minds of many today as the founder of the China Inland Mission. It is easy to forget that he became such by reason of his message. The Mission may be regarded as a sign of his apostleship, but the organization is only the outward expression of the truths he uttered. It is the embodiment of his teaching. The visible grew out of the invisible, the seen out of the unseen. Every world or cosmos is really framed by the Word of God, 'so that what is seen hath not been made out of things which do appear'. It is said that in Pretoria there is a hidden spring which supplies the whole community with water, and that the city has in fact been built around that bountiful supply. The buildings make a goodly show, but one secret at least of their existence is that inconspicuous fountain-head. And the China Inland Mission has grown up around the everflowing springs of God's Word. It came into being because of the creative energy of God's promises, and it is upheld by the same power. This is a truth we dare not forget. Hudson Taylor, the founder, is not with us now, but the promises of God's Word remain. We desire to remember the word he spoke.

There is no escaping the simple, downright purport of his words. With Paul and with the Psalmist he could say: 'I believed, and therefore did I speak.' If there was one thing more than another that characterised his utterances it was the genuine and authentic note of faith in God's Word. He believed it meant just what it said. And there was no evading the practical application of his faith. 'May God make our meditation very practical,' he would say, or 'What is needed is the humble, prayerful meditation of those who are determined to do the will of God'. 'The Bible is intended to teach us what God would have us *do*,' was another of his pointed observations. Like a nail in a sure place he drove this home. He was no doctrinaire, but an eminently practical teacher, as well as a practitioner himself. 'When will it dawn on the Lord's people', he almost cried, 'that God's command to preach the Gospel to every creature was not intended for the waste-paper basket?' It was impossible not to be arrested by such forceful speaking. Assent he knew was all too fatally easy. It was obedience God demanded.

Macaulay has spoken of Bunyan as a man with 'an intimate knowledge of the English Bible, and a vast and dearly-bought spiritual experience'. This was also true of Hudson Taylor, though in some things he differed greatly from the famous dreamer. He had a remarkably deep and detailed familiarity with God's Word, together with a personal and hardly-won experience.

Speaking of Bunyan's Christian, another historian has said: 'That lonely figure, with the book and the burden and the lamentable cry, is not only Bunyan himself. It is also the representative Puritan of the English Puritan epoch, that epoch of which Bunyan was the faithful mirror in literature, as Cromwell in action.' Hudson Taylor also was an outstanding figure with the book, a burden and a cry, but it was in the new era of the Foreign Missionary Enterprise. The book was the same, but the burden and the cry were different. His burden was the spiritual need and claims of unnumbered millions still living in the City of Destruction, and his cry was for willing, skilful labourers who would enter these unevangelized regions with the message of Salvation. What that book was to him this little volume will in part reveal. It was his *vade-mecum*, food for his soul, a lamp to his feet, a guarantee of God's care, a foundation upon which to build, and God's armoury whence 'the man of God may be perfect, thoroughly furnished unto all good works'.

25

Scattered throughout the pages of back numbers of *China's Millions*, and other publications, now out of print, are still to be found many articles written by Mr. Taylor in the midst of the battle and born out of the stress and travail of his soul. Like many of the precious stones of nature they are the fruit of his own sufferings and trials. Ruskin in his *Ethics of the Dust* has a most suggestive chapter entitled *Crystal Sorrows*. Here he tells us that 'the torture and grieving of the earth seem necessary to bring out its full energy', that the marble slabs which delight our eyes and are the wealth of architecture, are 'precisely those on which the signs and brands of these earth-agonies have been chiefly struck', that 'there is not a purple vein nor flaming zone among them, which is not the record of their ancient torture'.

The value of Hudson Taylor's expositions is largely in consequence of his own heart-searching experiences, of trials which almost crushed him, and of crises which threatened to overwhelm him. As with the marble, so with the man. 'There are things that even God cannot do for us unless He allows us to suffer. He cannot have the result of a process without the process.'

Isaac Newton is reported to have said that the only difference between himself and other men was that he looked more, and therefore saw more. Eyes alone do not make us see. They are only the instruments of sight. The question is, What made Newton look more? Hudson Taylor saw more in God's Word than many men because he looked more. His great adventure for God, his hunger for the souls of men, as well as for his own soul in the midst of his quest, compelled him to look more deeply and to look more eagerly into God's Word. And not only did he see more, but he had the wondrous faculty of 'adding a precious seeing to the eye and to the mind' of others. This again makes his expositions worth conserving.

Another characteristic of Hudson Taylor's expositions is their crystal clearness. Profundity and simplicity are not incompatibles. 'In matters of religion,' wrote Milton, 'he is learnedest who is plainest.' The river of God is full of water, and the 'river of the water of life' is 'clear as crystal'. Hudson Taylor, who drank freely of this river, was an illustration of this. He was well-learned in the things of God, yet he could convey his meaning with great plainness of speech. His school had been the school of realities. There was no need to be obscure and abstract. He did not treat of academic theories, but of convictions which had been tempered in the furnace of affliction. His pictures were never blurred or out of focus. The glass of experience gave good definition to all his persuasions. The humblest reader cannot miss the meaning.

From the legacy of his message the following thirty short readings have been selected. They are words we would not willingly let die.

'Made like unto His brethren'[1]

It behoved Him in all things to be made like unto His brethren
(Hebrews 2:17).

I have never heard of anyone who, after having *bona fide*
attempted to become Chinese to the Chinese, that he might gain
the Chinese, either regretted the step he had taken, or desired to
abandon the course. Merely to put on their dress, and yet to act
regardless of their thoughts and feelings, is to make a burlesque
of the whole matter. Let us appeal to the Word of God. Consider
the Apostle and High Priest of our profession, Christ Jesus, who
was faithful to Him who appointed Him, and left us an
example that we should follow in His steps.

Had our Lord appeared on earth as an angel of light, He would
doubtless have inspired far more awe and reverence, and would
have collected together even larger multitudes to attend His
ministry. But to save man He became Man, not merely like man,
but *very* man. In language, in costume, in everything unsinful,
He made Himself one with those He sought to benefit. Had He
been born a noble Roman, rather than a Jew, He would, perhaps,
if less loved, have commanded more of a certain kind of respect;
and He would assuredly thereby have been spared much indignity
to which He was subjected. This, however, was not His aim; He
emptied Himself.

Surely no follower of the meek and lowly Jesus will be likely
to conclude that it is 'beneath the dignity of a Christian
missionary' to seek identification with this poor people, in the
hope that he may see them washed, sanctified, and justified in
the name of the Lord Jesus, and by the Spirit of our God! Let us
rather be followers of Him who 'knowing that the Father had
given all things into His hands, and that He was come from God,
and went to God, He riseth from supper, and laid aside His

---

1. From a paper written for candidates not later than 1868.

28

garments, and took a towel, and girded Himself. After that He poured water into a basin, and began to wash the disciples' feet, and to wipe them with the towel wherewith He was girded.'

'Servant unto All'

Though I be free from all men, yet I made myself servant unto all, that I might gain the more (1 Corinthians 9:19).

We have a beautiful commentary on the life of the Lord Jesus in that of him who could truthfully say: 'To me to live is Christ'. This greatest of all missionaries tells us in what spirit he achieved his wonderful successes: 'Though I be free from all men, yet have I made myself servant unto all, that I might gain the more.... And this I do for the Gospel's sake.'

We conceive that no amplification is needed to convince any unprejudiced mind of the soundness of the principle here stated; but the question may arise as to how far it is applicable to the Chinese. We have to do with a people whose prejudices in favour of their own customs and habits are the growth of ages and millenniums. The chief objection that prince and people have against Christianity is, that it is a *foreign* religion, and that its tendencies are to approximate believers to foreign nations. I am not peculiar in holding the opinion that the foreign dress and carriage of missionaries – to a certain extent affected by some of their converts and pupils – the foreign appearance of the chapels and, indeed, the foreign air given to everything connected with religion, have very largely hindered the rapid dissemination of the truth among the Chinese. But why should such a foreign aspect be given to Christianity? The Word of God does not require it; nor, I conceive, could sound reason justify it. It is not their denationalization, but their Christianization that we seek. We wish to see Christian Chinamen and Chinawomen, true Christians, but withal true Chinese in every sense of the word. We wish to see Churches of Christian Chinese presided over by Chinese pastors and officers, worshipping in edifices of a thoroughly Chinese style of architecture. If we really desire to see the Chinese such as we have described, let us, as far as possible, set before them a correct example. Let us, in everything not sinful, become Chinese, that by all means we may win some.

'Let This Mind Be in You'[1]

> Who being in the form of God, counted it not a prize
> to be on an equality with God, but emptied Himself,
> taking the form of a servant (Philippians 2:6-7).

'Ye know the grace of our Lord Jesus Christ, that, though He was rich, yet for your sakes He became poor, that ye through His poverty might be rich.' 'Let this mind be in you.'

Will any one reflect on what He gave up who left Heaven's throne to be cradled in a manger; who, having filled all things and wielded omnipotence, became a feeble infant and was wrapped in swaddling clothes; who being the Loved One of the Father, never unappreciated, never misunderstood, and receiving the ceaseless adoration of the hierarchies of heaven, became a despised Nazarene, misunderstood by His most faithful followers, suspected by those whom He came to bless, neglected and rejected by those who owed to Him their very being, and whose salvation He had come to seek; and, finally, mocked and spit upon, crucified and slain, with thieves, bandits and outlaws. Will, I ask, any brother or sister reflect on this, and yet hesitate to make the trifling sacrifices to which we have alluded? We give you credit, dear friends, for being prepared to give up not only these little things, but a thousand more for Christ. We believe it is your desire, through grace, not to count your lives dear unto yourselves, that you may finish your course with joy and the ministry which you receive from the Lord Jesus.

Let there be no reservation: give yourself up wholly and fully to Him whose you are, and whom you wish to serve in this work, and then there can be no disappointment. But once let the question arise, 'Are we *called* to give up this, or that, or the other?' or admit the thought, 'I did not expect this or that privation or inconvenience, and your service will cease to be that free and happy one which is most conducive to efficiency and success. 'God loveth a cheerful giver.'

---

1. From a paper written not later than 1868 for candidates.

1. The Secret of Success

> Glory to God in the highest, and on earth peace,
> goodwill toward men (Luke 2:14).

Four thousand years had man been vainly struggling and striving when the Deliverer came. How the angels rejoiced as God laid help on One that was mighty – almighty. The world was lying in the wicked one: Satan's triumph seemed almost complete. Then God undertook to save – at His own time, in His own way, and for His own glory. Soon the glad tidings are noised abroad – 'Unto you is born this day, in the city of David, a Saviour, which is Christ the Lord. His name shall be called Wonderful, Counsellor, The Mighty God, The Everlasting Father, The Prince of Peace.' Well may we ask, when and how did He come, and how did He undertake His mighty and glorious task?

Did He come when earth's brightest sun was shining with all its noontide splendour, and pale its glory by His own superior effulgence, while the awe-struck nobles of this earth vied with each other in welcoming Him with more than royal honours? No! In the quiet hours of the night, without pomp, and without observation, the Lord of glory stole, as it were, unseen into this sin-stricken world.

Where is He, where is He that is born King of the Jews? demand the wise men at Jerusalem. Search the halls of the great, the homes of the wise, the palaces of the noble! But no; He is not there! Yet, surely, He must be found in the city of the great King! Nay, Jerusalem shelters Him not! Would you find Him? Go to Bethlehem-Ephratah, the little one of the thousands of Judah, and even there you will find Him lying in a manger – for there was no room for Him and His parents in the inn.

Not to Herod on his throne was the angelic vision vouchsafed; nor to the High Priest, nor to the Sanhedrin was this revelation given, nor even to the seeking Magi; but to humble shepherds, keeping their watch by night. And still there are many revelations for the faithful toiler that ease and luxury will never know.

2. The Secret of Success

Jesus therefore said to them again, Peace be unto you: as the
Father hath sent Me, even so send I you (John 20:21).

The heavenly hosts had sung with wondering gladness when
chaos was clothed with beauty; and the work of creation was
completed. But now they see with greater wonder the Creator
Himself veiled in human form and self-emptied, lying in a
manger. They knew the grace of our Lord, as never before, when
they saw Him as Jesus Christ, who 'though He was rich, yet for
our sakes became poor'. The Wisdom of God, and the Power of
God has undertaken our deliverance, and in order to accomplish
it seeks no alliance with the wisdom, the wealth, the nobility of
earth, but *intelligently takes* the lowest place as that *best adapted*
for carrying out His purposes of love and grace.

Have we learnt this lesson? Are we willing to learn it? 'As
the Father hath sent Me into the world, even so send I you.' Or,
are we going to repeat the oft-made experiment – which has
always failed and always must fail – of trying to improve upon
God's plan? The poverty and weakness of apostolic missions
necessitated reliance upon God alone and issued in wonderful
success, and in modern missions it will invariably be found that
in proportion to the non-reliance on wealth, or education, or
political power, and in proportion to the self-emptying with which
they are carried on, the issues are encouraging. The persecutions
of Burmah and Madagascar, and the dangers of labours among
the cannibals of the South Sea Islands have proved no barrier to
success, but have been conditions of blessing.

Can those who at home or abroad are ambitious for the
highest success as fishers of men find a wiser or safer example
than that of Him who called His first disciples to leave all and
follow Him, and who Himself, 'though He was rich, yet for our
sakes became poor'?

1. Spiritual Science

Ye know the grace of our Lord Jesus Christ, that, though He
was rich, yet for your sakes He became poor, that ye through
His poverty might become rich (2 Corinthians 8:9).

There is a natural science of which wise men avail themselves,
and by which they accomplish great results unheard of by our
forefathers. Our God is the God of nature as well as of grace;
and as He always acts in the *best* way, so, in the same
circumstances, He always acts in the *same* way. The uniformity
of His mode of action in nature is seen and recognized by many
who do not know the great Actor. Such often prefer to speak of
the constancy of the laws of nature, rather than of the uniformity
of the operations of God. But if we speak of the laws of nature,
let us not misunderstand the expression. It is the law of a well-
regulated household that the door is opened when the door-bell
is rung. It would be an entire mistake, however, to suppose that
this is *done* by the law: it is done, no matter whether directly or
mediately, by the head of the household. So a sparrow 'shall
not fall on the ground without your Father'.

We who know God, and are His children, do well to remind
ourselves that it is *our unchanging* God who makes the water
on the fire to boil, and the steam in the engine to develop such
expansive power; that it is He who acts uniformly in electricity,
whether we avail ourselves of His power in the useful telegraph,
or succumb to it in the fatal thunderbolt; and that it is *His uniform
action* that we recognize as the law of gravitation.

No less constant and sovereign is He in the domain of grace:
His sovereignty is never erratic or arbitrary. His method of action
may be studied and largely discovered in spiritual things as in
natural. Some of His laws are plainly revealed in His Word; others
are exemplified in the actions recorded therein. And best of all,
by the illumination of the Holy Ghost, God Himself may be
known, and loved, and revered, through the study of His written
Word; and He is especially seen in the face of Jesus Christ.

2. Spiritual Science

Ye know the grace of our Lord Jesus Christ, that, though He
was rich, yet for your sakes He became poor, that ye through
His poverty might become rich (2 Corinthians 8:9).

The indispensable illumination of the Holy Ghost is never denied
to those who seek it, and are honestly desirous to have it *on
God's own terms*. Spiritual things can only be spiritually
discerned; but those who are spiritual have no more difficulty
in learning spiritual laws (by which we mean God's uniform
mode of acting in the same circumstances in spiritual things),
than natural men have in learning natural laws. Nay, in spiritual
things there is less difficulty, for they are revealed more clearly:
research into the Word and ways of God more readily shows us
His modes of action than research and observation do in natural
science. Some of the secrets of grace may be known by all the
children of God, if they are *willing* to be taught, and be *obedient*
as they are taught.

As in natural things there are many mysteries beyond the ken
of feeble man, so also in spiritual things there are things not yet
revealed, not intended to be known here and now. But just as by
utilizing what may be known, and is known in nature, men achieve
great results – as by steam, electricity, etc. – so by utilizing what
is revealed and may be known in spiritual things great results
may be achieved. Ten thousand horses could not convey the loads
from London to Glasgow in a week that are easily taken in half a
day by rail; ten thousand couriers could not convey the tidings
from London to Shanghai in months that may be flashed by cable
in a few hours. And so in spiritual things no amount of labour
and machinery will accomplish without spiritual power, what
may easily be accomplished when we place ourselves in the
current of God's will, and work by His direction, in His way.

3. Spiritual Science

> Ye know the grace of our Lord Jesus Christ, that, though He
> was rich, yet for your sakes He became poor, that ye through
> His poverty might become rich (2 Corinthians 8:9).

There are also conditions of success in spiritual things. Ignoring these, we may toil much, sow much, and reap little. Has not the failure of many of our efforts been due to our attempting to do God's work in man's way – aye, and sometimes even in the devil's way? Does this seem a startling question? Just read the account of the temptations of our Lord, after His baptism, and see what Satan's ways are. Have they not *often* been used, unknowingly, to forward work for God? Have not Christians at home and native helpers in foreign lands often been induced to *begin* work, and perhaps still more often to *continue* work, by inducements of support and position? Would the same sums of money always be contributed if the plate were not passed, or if the donors' names were not published?

When the Lord of glory came to bring the highest blessing, He chose the lowest place, as that best adapted to accomplish His purpose. In like manner *in order to enrich us*, poor bankrupts, He intelligently and cheerfully *emptied Himself* of all His riches, as neither needed nor suited to effect His purpose. We do well to remember that He was the *Wisdom* of God, and the *Power* of God, and necessarily chose the *wisest* way, and the *mightiest* way to effect His purpose. He might have become incarnate as a noble Roman; He would doubtless have gained disciples by it – but of what kind? Or He might have come into the family of a noble and wealthy Jew; but He did not – that was not God's way.

The Corinthian Christians knew the grace of the Lord Jesus Christ, that though He was rich, yet for their sakes He became poor. Do we? Do we want to know it? Are we 'imitators of God' if we make no costly sacrifices for the salvation of men? It is our Isaacs who are wanted for the altar, not our superfluities. Are we followers of Christ if we do not walk in love, as Christ also loved us, and gave Himself up for us?

Lessons from the Incarnation

Forasmuch, then, as the children are partakers of flesh and
blood, He also Himself likewise took part of the same
(Hebrews 2:14).

The incarnation of our Lord and Saviour Jesus Christ is full of
blessed teaching – teaching specially instructive to those who wish
to follow Him in rescuing the perishing. The story is a wonderful
one. Let us consider its bearings on practical Christian work. In
what way can we become followers of Christ in His incarnation?

As we aim at being fruitful, we find our need of intelligent
understanding of the divine methods, in order that we may apply
them in our own work. We have seen that the Lord Jesus
humbled Himself, and took the lowest place when He came to
raise us; and we have dwelt upon the fact that He emptied Himself
that we might be made rich. We would fain learn, however, not
only what He laid aside, but what He put on, the better to fit
Himself for successful ministry. We are told that the Word was
made flesh and dwelt among us, that He was found in fashion as
a man, that He took upon Him the form of a servant. While never
forgetting His Divine nature, He never used it to resist the powers
of evil, to supply His personal needs, or to claim immunities for
Himself or His disciples. He steadfastly maintained His position
of being in all things like unto His brethren – a lesson too much
forgotten in missionary service.

The Christian missionary has no heaven to leave, no divinity
to lay aside; but, as a rule, he leaves a home. He has a nationality
which he may claim, and through which he may obtain many
immunities for himself and his followers; or he may see it wiser
to suffer than to do so. He may claim the status of a foreigner, or
he may assimilate himself in dress, appearance, home, language to
those around him. Nothing is easier than to find objections to
this course; but it was the course that Jesus did take, and we are
persuaded would still have us take. The Master says: 'I have
given you an example, that ye should do as I have done unto you.'

10th Day

1. Apostolic Example

Be ye followers of me, even as I also am of Christ
(1 Corinthians 11:1).

If any are perplexed by the question, sometimes raised, as to whether the self-emptying life of the Lord Jesus was not a necessity of His atoning work rather than an example for service, no such difficulty attends the life of the great missionary apostle. To few have such personal manifestations of Christ been granted, and by few has His life been as faithfully reproduced.

What was the effect of the revelation of Christ on the Apostle Paul? Immediately after his enlightenment he so preached Christ as to share in His reproach and rejection. He determined to know nothing but Jesus Christ, and Him *crucified*. He emptied himself as far as it was possible for any man to do so. Advantages of birth, of position, of education – in a word, what things soever were gain to him, those he counted *loss* for Christ; and glad he was, in spiritual barter, to count them all as loss, and dross, and dung, for the excellency of the knowledge of Christ Jesus his Lord.

Suppose that, instead, he had envied a Roman villa, and frescoed walls, and marble fountains, and statuettes – had sought for and obtained a courtier's position and a courtier's crown – would he have been the gainer or the loser? Had he not in life a moral dignity of far greater value – a spiritual joy infinitely transcending the pleasures of the world? Is not his life exercising a mighty effect even today, after the lapse of eighteen centuries? And are not all these things, grand as they are, utterly eclipsed by the glorious welcome the Christian hero received when the sword of Nero liberated his enfranchised spirit for its triumphant entry into the presence of the King? Ah! His 'Well done!' was a glorious reward, not bought too dearly by a life of poverty and toil and service below. Do we not still hear the echo of his words: 'Be ye followers of me, as I also am of Christ?'

11th Day

2. Apostolic Example

Be ye followers of me, even as I also am of Christ
(1 Corinthians 11:1).

It pleased God when He called the apostle Paul to take his first missionary journey, to select for him a companion – Barnabas, 'the son of consolation'. When he obtained this designation we do not know; but a very characteristic event is recorded of him in the fourth chapter of the Acts. There we find him, as one who was rich, for the sake of his impoverished and tried brethren voluntarily becoming poor, in order that he might succour and comfort them. Did he not thus become a son of consolation? How poor he became we may learn from the words of the Apostle Paul, from which it appears that, he, like Paul, laboured with his own hands.

These were the men whom God saw fit to honour with the *first place* on the long roll of missionaries of Christ – these were the men through whose ministry church after church sprang up – these were the men whom no danger could daunt, whom Jewish religiousness and Gentile superstition essayed in vain to silence and overcome.

Let us note also that these apostles went about their work in the same way that their Lord and Master had done. He coming to men became man, and being personally sent to the Jews, He became a Jew. The apostle, on the other hand, being already a Jew, had to labour especially among the Gentiles. Did he then live among them after the manner of the Jews? Or did he, as far as possible, assimilate himself to the objects of his ministry? He answers this question himself in 1 Corinthians 9:19-23: 'Though I be free from all men, yet have I made myself servant unto all, that I might win the more.... I became all things to all men, that I might by all means save some. And this I do for the Gospel's sake.'

It is noteworthy that after this remarkable declaration the

Holy Spirit, by the Apostle, exhorts us likewise to 'so run that ye may obtain'. We confidently believe that there is a secret here which would often have spared tried workers the disappointment of years of unsuccessful labour.

Who Were the Losers?

He that withholdeth corn, the people shall curse him: but
blessing shall be upon the head of him that selleth it
(Proverbs 11:26).

History repeats itself. Eighteen hundred years ago there was a
widespread impression that a coming Messiah would soon appear,
and a few were earnestly waiting for the redemption of Israel. He
did appear. He lived and died, He rose again and shed forth the
promise of the Father, the Holy Ghost, on those He left behind as
His representatives.

Strange was the effect this produced. The disciples began to
think that Jesus *meant* what He *said; and they acted on His
directions*. They began to love as brethren; to sell that which
they had, and give alms. No member of the Church had any
lack. Doubtless many of the wise ones of this world spoke
scornfully of such fanaticism, and folly, and prided themselves
on their own possessions, determining to 'leave the rest of their
substance to their babes'. But *did they do so*?

A few years rolled on, and, as foretold by the Master,
troublous times came. Jerusalem was compassed with armies.
*The day for selling possessions and using the proceeds for Jesus
was past*. Many of the faithful believers were far away preaching
the Gospel in distant parts. Of those who escaped from
Jerusalem, some may have spent their all in the service of their
Master, and thus had nothing to leave. Others, though obedient
to His warning to flee, had perhaps been more 'prudent', and
had retained somewhat of their possessions for a rainy day. *Who
were the losers?* Again, some members of the Church, perhaps,
abode by their stuff in Jerusalem, instead of fleeing to the
mountains. Again I ask: *Who were the losers?*

History repeats itself. The coming of the Lord draweth nigh.
In that day who will be the losers? Who are the followers of Him
who laid *all* He was and *all* He had upon the altar? Who emptied
Himself, giving His life a ransom for many? *Will they be the losers?*

1. Divine Possession and Government

When Israel went forth out of Egypt, the house of Jacob from
a people of strange language; Judah became His sanctuary,
Israel His dominion (Psalm 114:1, 2).

'When Israel went forth out of Egypt!' But why did they go in?
It would be easy to reply, that the famine compelled them to do
so. But this would only raise the further question – Why was the
famine sent? We must look deeper than this. Israel failed in the
land of promise. One of his last utterances in that land abundantly
shows this: 'All these things are against me.' Poor Jacob! He has
had many successors; and not a few have gone down from the land
of promise into the land of bondage. It is in the land of Egypt, and
not in Canaan, that we find Jacob using the words: 'The God before
whom my fathers Abraham and Isaac did walk, the God which
hath fed (lit. *shepherded*) me all my life long unto this day, the
Angel which hath redeemed me from all evil, bless the lads'.

The beginning of the sojourn in Egypt promised well; but
hard was the bondage in which it terminated. It seemed hopeless
too; from within there was no power to deliver; from without
no power to pity and redeem. Had such a people as Israel not
been taken down into Egypt, and kept separate, they would have
mingled with the Canaanites, and lost the privilege of being
dwelt among, and governed by, the great I AM.

Kept there until the fulness of time, it was equally necessary
to bring them out: for it is not written: 'while Israel was *in* Egypt',
but, 'when Israel went forth *out* of Egypt, Judah became His
sanctuary, and Israel His dominion'. Their coming out of Egypt
was unmistakably necessary.

The power of Egypt was proved impotent to resist; the
unwilling people were made willing in the day of His power; and
under the leadership of Joshua, was fully accomplished that which
by the hand of Moses was commenced, and the chosen people
entered into possession of the promised land. 'Judah became His
sanctuary; Israel His dominion.'

2. Divine Possession and Government

Judah became His sanctuary, Israel His dominion (Psalm 114:2).

How was this glorious issue brought about? It was not the matter of Moses, the leader; of Aaron, the priest; or of Joshua, the faithful servant and successful general. Their names are not even mentioned in this Psalm. Nor was it a question of the docility of Israel, or of their apprehension of the relationship which the great God condescended to bear to the chosen nation. It was the great and glorious *fact* that *He* took possession of Judah, and, coming down among them, sanctified them by His presence. It was the great *fact* that, willing or unwilling, *He* claimed Israel and made Israel His dominion, and governed them for their good – oft times in spite of themselves – that led to this glorious issue.

Little did the tribe of Judah apprehend the greatness of that glorious One who humbled Himself to dwell among them, and who in due course became incarnate in their royal house. Little did they realize the honour conferred upon themselves by His presence. Little did they practically rise to the dignity and sanctity becoming those who were indwelt by the Holy One. But the *fact* remained, despite their failure to apprehend it; and, notwithstanding all the hindrances and delays caused by unbelief, it secured the ultimate fulfilment of God's covenant promise.

Nor was it the tribe of Judah alone that was taken up; God laid hold of the whole nation. God had become their God, and they nationally had become His dominion – *from His side*. The possession of Canaan was secured to the nation by the *fact* that Israel had become His dominion.

But what happiness the people missed! What hills of iron and brass, and valleys of milk and honey they might have possessed and enjoyed, instead of wandering, weary and hopeless, in the dreary wilderness, which ultimately became their grave, as they perished one by one. How solemn a lesson is their fate for us. He *wills* to save.

3. Divine Possession and Government

The sea saw it and fled; Jordan was driven back. The mountains skipped like rams, the little hills like lambs (Psalm 114:3, 4).

Judah as we have seen, sadly failed to apprehend God's presence in their midst, and Israel proved both faithless and insubordinate. But all this did not annul the *fact* that Israel had a King, and that King a mighty One. Strange that man alone should resist His Maker. But blessed is the truth that His presence is not dependent upon our apprehension of it, nor His power to save necessarily limited by our want of faith. 'The sea saw it and fled; Jordan was driven back.'

But if this was the case, despite the sin and failure of the people, what would have been the blessing had faith been in lively exercise? Blessed is he who gives up his whole being to his Saviour and his God, for His indwelling and governance.

Apart from this His indwelling and governance how truly helpless we are, and how ofttimes hopeless we become! But how changed all this becomes when it is no longer 'I', but 'Christ', who 'liveth in me'! Then, we do not cry to be delivered *out* of the body of this death, but the life that we live – though still *in* the flesh – we live in the faith (faithfulness) of the Son of God, who loved us, and gave Himself for us.

We shall not find this new life a life without conflict. The world still remains the world; the flesh still remains the flesh; the devil still remains the devil. Escaped from Egypt, Egypt will pursue us; but whereas the Red Sea would prove an insuperable barrier to the carnal mind, if Christ be indwelling, the sea sees it and flees, and we begin to find that there is *no hindrance in the presence of our Master and King*. The proud waves of the sea, the swellings of Jordan overflowing its banks, own the presence of Him, who when on earth calmed the fears of the fishermen on the Sea of Galilee, and said: 'Peace, be still!' to the raging waves. Mountains of difficulty skip out of the way like rams; and the more numerous little hills in His presence become harmless as lambs.

4. Divine Possession and Government

The sea saw it and fled; Jordan was driven back. The mountains skipped like rams, the little hills like lambs (Psalm 114:3, 4).

Is it not just when assured of God's indwelling presence, and we count it all joy when we fall into divers temptations, that we begin to realize that for us all things really do work together for good. Then we begin to sing, before the battle, the song of praise in anticipation of the rich spoils of which we are assured. The intelligent believer would not lose the conflicts; for apart from them, where would be the psalm?

In the history of the bringing out of Israel from Egypt, and of their bringing in to the promised land, as detailed in the Pentateuch and in Joshua, the principal instruments used by God are brought frequently before us. But they find no place in this psalm. We are brought directly into the presence of God, and human agency disappears. Nor is this all. We find no mention of the wilderness – it disappears with the faithless generation who were buried in it. Why is this? Because in the life of faith there is no wilderness. The sea – the boundary on this side – sees our Master and flees; Jordan – the boundary on that side – in His presence is driven back. The wilderness is for unbelievers, who *will not* enter into rest.

Not a little misleading are some of our popular hymns, which compare Jordan with death, and Canaan with heaven. What! after we get to heaven shall we have to fight every step of our way, slaughtering the inhabitants, ere we can enter into the prepared mansions? No! Ten thousand times, No! The Canaan rest is to be enjoyed *now*; and, under our victorious Joshua, each battle *should* result in victory, and every foe *should* be dispossessed and put down. We have advisedly said *should*; for, if Achan rob God, defeat will follow; and if instead of putting down the Canaanites, we begin to make truces with them, we shall end by being driven out.

And this brings us to two very practical questions. Where are we? In bondage? In the wilderness? Or in the restful land? And, if in the land, are our victories hindered by any compromise with the foes of God?

5. Divine Possession and Government

What aileth thee, O thou sea, that thou fleest? Thou Jordan, that thou turnest back? Ye mountains, that ye skip like rams; Ye little hills, like lambs? Tremble, thou earth, at the presence of the
    Lord, at the presence of the God of Jacob (Psalm 114:5-7).

We have been brought into the goodly land; the mountains and the little hills alike proved no barriers. We lost sight of the human agency in the presence of the Master; and there remained no wilderness. Even those earthly blessings which are His own good gift He often sees fit to remove. He has promised – *promised* not threatened: 'Yet once more will I make to tremble, not the earth only, but also the heaven. And this word, *Yet once more*, signifieth the removing of those things that are shaken, as of things which have been made, that those things which are not shaken may remain.' Perhaps sometimes we fail to realize how great a cause for thankfulness we have, when a loving Father removes some prop that can be shaken, on which we are leaning all too fondly, instead of resting alone on the Rock of Ages – a prop which was to some extent eclipsing to our view the Kingdom which cannot be shaken. Perhaps He saw that we were too content to rest on our oars, and trust to some mooring-post, which prevented us, indeed, from drifting with the current, but was incompatible with our making progress upstream, and with that arduous battling with the wild waters around, which was a needful training for future victories. There is a day coming in which not only will the sea flee and Jordan be turned back, but heaven and earth will flee away at the presence of Him who is now known to us as the Lord, the God of Jacob. It is with this Mighty One we have to do, not with mountains and hills, rivers or seas. May we not well be content with *any* circumstances, and *any* surroundings, when He has said: 'I will in no wise fail thee, neither will I in any wise forsake thee'. With 'good courage' we may say: 'The Lord is my Helper, I will not fear; what shall man do unto me?'

6. Divine Possession and Government

Tremble, thou earth, at the presence of the Lord, at the presence of the God of Jacob; Which turned the rock into a pool of water, the flint into a fountain of waters (Psalm 114:7-8).

For the encouragement of His faithful ones there is no *mention* of the wilderness in this Psalm. And yet, for the encouragement of the timid and the desponding, there are cheering *allusions* to it, especially in the last verse. For it was in the wilderness that the rock became a pool of water, and the flint was turned into a fountain of waters. Is there not also very much tender consideration in the only titles given to our God in this Psalm – the Lord (not in capitals), and the God of Jacob. Conscious, perhaps, that we have not the faith of Abraham, nor even that of Caleb and Joshua, God draws near to us as the Lord, and not as Jehovah, and as the God of poor, faltering and failing Jacob; and if any of us dare not claim to be in the land and fear that we are still in the waste, howling wilderness, are we not reassured as we think of Him who promised to be with Jacob in all his wanderings? Then were the gracious words spoken: 'Behold, I am with thee, and will keep thee whithersoever thou goest, and will bring thee again into this land; for I will not leave thee, until I have done that which I have spoken to thee of.'

Not altogether dissimilar to the words of this Psalm were the encouragements given to John the Baptist for the preparatory work which he was sent to do: 'Every valley shall be filled, and every mountain and hill shall be brought low.' In carrying on the work we are commissioned to do, we have our seas and rivers to cross, or mountains and hills to surmount and remove. In our own strength we might well look upon our task as hopeless, and our efforts as labour lost. But if each worker realizes himself as a temple of the living God, an instrument possessed and governed and used by the Almighty, there is no place for discouragement. Before Him, the hard, dry rock shall be turned into a pool, the flint into a fountain of water.

Considering the Poor

> Blessed is he that considereth the poor: The LORD
> will deliver him in the day of evil (Psalm 41:1).

This man's character so resembles that of Christ, that God 'considers' him with favour. He has beheld as in a glass the features of his Lord, and like a glass reflects His character. The heart of God goes out towards him, and every needful good is bestowed. Is he in trouble, who has considered, and to the extent of his ability helped, those in trouble? Will God do less for him? No! 'The Lord will deliver him in time of trouble; the Lord will preserve him and keep him alive, and he shall be blessed.'

But who is the one so blessed? Not the one who cheaply relieves his own eyes of a painful spectacle by a trifling alms, or relieves himself of the importunity of a collector for some benevolent cause. Not the one who quiets his own conscience by gifts which really cost no self-denial, and then dismisses the case of the poor and needy from his thoughts, complacently claiming the blessings promised to the charitable. As for those who seek fame and name by their gifts, we altogether dismiss their case from consideration. The blessing is pronounced on those who *consider* the poor, who turn their thoughts and attention towards the poor and needy and who do what they can, at the cost of personal self-denial, to lessen the sum of human woe. Such *are* blessed indeed, and such *shall* be blessed: blessing is their inalienable portion.

Do not let us spiritualize the text so as to lose its obvious character. This we Protestants are often in no small danger of doing. How much of the precious time and strength of our Lord was spent in conferring temporal blessing on the poor, the afflicted, and the needy? Such ministrations, proceeding from right motives, cannot be lost. They are Godlike; they are Christlike.

We pen these lines in a Chinese boat, moored by a Chinese village. My heart is full; what shall I say? I implore you to consider the case of these poor, and may the Lord give you understanding.

> God hath spoken once; twice have I heard this,
> that power belongeth unto God (Psalm 62:11).

God Himself is the great source of power. It is His possession. 'Power belongeth unto God', and He manifests it according to His sovereign will. Yet, not in an erratic or arbitrary manner, but according to His declared purpose and promises. True, our opponents and hindrances are many and mighty, but our God, the living God, is Almighty.

God tells us by His prophet Daniel, that the people who do know their God shall be strong and do exploits. It is ordinarily true that knowledge is power, it is supremely true in the case of the knowledge of God. Those who know their God do not *attempt* to do exploits, but *do* them. We shall search the Scriptures in vain for any command to *attempt* to do anything. God's commands are always 'Do this'. If the command be from God, our only course is to obey. Further, God's power is available power. We are supernatural people, born again by a supernatural birth, kept by a supernatural power, sustained on supernatural food, taught by a supernatural Teacher from a supernatural Book. We are led by a supernatural Captain in right paths to assured victories. The risen Saviour, ere He ascended on high, said, 'All power is given unto Me. Go ye therefore'.

Again, He said to His disciples: 'Ye shall receive power when the Holy Spirit is come upon you.' Not many days after this, in answer to united and continued prayer, the Holy Spirit did come upon them, and they were all filled. Praise God, He remains with us still. The power given is not a gift from the Holy Spirit. He Himself is the power. Today He is as truly available, and as mighty in power, as He was on the day of Pentecost. But since the days before Pentecost, has the whole Church ever put aside every other work, and waited upon God for ten days, that that power might be manifested? We have given too much attention to method, and to machinery, and to resources, and too little to the source of power.

What Wilt Thou?

Then Jesus answered and said unto her, O woman, great is thy
faith: be it unto thee even as thou wilt (Matthew 15:28).

By faith the walls of Jericho fell down – yet what more unlikely!
We walk by faith. Do we? What record is there on high of things
that by faith we have obtained? Is each step each day an act of
faith? Do we, as children of God, really believe the Bible? Are
we ready to take the place of even a worm, as our Master did –
'But I am a worm and no man'? Or if we realize our powerlessness
and our insignificance, do we believe that it is possible – that it is
God's will for us – that we should thresh mountains? 'Fear not,'
said the Lord by the prophet of old, 'fear not, thou worm Jacob,...
behold I will make thee a sharp threshing instrument having teeth:
thou shalt thresh the mountains and beat them small, and shalt
make the hills as chaff. Thou shalt fan them, and the wind shall
carry them away, and the whirlwind shall scatter them: and thou
shalt rejoice in the Lord, and shalt glory in the Holy One of Israel.'

How then, do we ask, are we to thresh mountains? Let us
listen to our Master: 'Have faith in God. For verily I say unto
you, That whosoever shall say unto this mountain, Be thou
removed, and be thou cast into the sea; and shall not doubt in
his heart, but shall believe that those things which he saith shall
come to pass, he shall have whatsoever he saith.' Do we ask
when this shall be? The Lord continues: 'What things soever ye
desire *when ye pray*, believe that ye receive them, and ye shall
have them'. Let us therefore 'be careful for nothing; but in
everything by prayer and supplication with thanksgiving, let
our requests be made known unto God'.

Now let us stop and ask ourselves: What do we desire? and
then let us claim the promise at once. Have we loved ones
unsaved? Have we difficulties to conquer? Have we mountains
to remove? Then let us take it to the Lord in prayer.

God's Pruning-Knife

> If a man abide not in Me, he is cast forth as a branch, and is withered; and men gather them, and cast them into the fire, and they are burned (John 15:6).

Elsewhere we have remarked that our Lord's teaching does not refer to the loss of the soul, but to the loss of the life, as an opportunity of fruit-bearing. In this verse He further points out that not only does the Father take the fruitless branch away, leaving it to wither, but that men gather them and cast them into the fire, and they are burned. How terribly true this often is. Oh, how scorching is the power of sin, and how blighted are the lives of many who perhaps are only restored with a death-bed repentance, saved as by fire! The world is a hard master; and sin, even if forgiven, is *never* undone; its consequences remain. The sin of David was forgiven, but the prophet who announced the pardon was commissioned to tell him that the sword should *never* depart from his house. Every sin committed is a seed sown, and abides in its consequences; and however secret it may have been, it shall, as the Saviour teaches, be brought to light.

This truth much needs emphasis in the present day, even among the children of God. The enormity of sin, and the awful consequences which result from it, are too little realized and too little taught. Because God graciously promises that forgiven sin shall no more be remembered against the believer, many forget that God's Word equally assures us that 'God shall bring every work into judgment, with every secret thing, whether it be good or whether it be evil' – a passage the force of which has not passed away under the new dispensation; for the Lord Himself endorses it, saying: 'There is nothing covered that shall not be revealed, and hid that shall not be known'. And Paul says: 'We must all appear before the judgment seat of Christ.'

And not only so; for even in this life there is a reaping, in measure, of that which is sown, which may come from the hands of men, who are oft-times God's sword to chasten His children.

Separation unto God

The vow of a Nazarite, to separate himself unto Jehovah
(Numbers 6:2, 4).

Much is revealed in this chapter in germ which is more fully
brought out in the New Testament. Under the Old Covenant
many blessings were enjoyed in measure and for a season, which
in this dispensation are ours in their fulness and permanence.
For instance, the Israelite might vow the vow of a Nazarite and
separate himself unto God for a season; but it is the privilege of
the Christian to know himself as always separated to God.

Israel might have been a kingdom of priests; but through their
own sin they had nationally forfeited this privilege. God, however,
opened a way for the individual who wished to draw near to Him
to do so. But it is important to note that the vow was only a
temporary consecration, yet it involved, while it lasted, an absolute
acceptance of the will of God. So, in the present day, God is
willing to give His people fulness of blessing, but it must be on
His own lines. Devotion to God is still a voluntary thing; hence
the difference of attainment among Christians. While salvation
is a free gift, the 'winning Christ' can only be through unreserved
and unquestioning obedience.

The obedience of Adam was tested in the Garden by the
prohibition of one tree – so was the obedience of the Nazarite
tested. It was not the thing that was harmful in itself, but the
doing the will of God, even in matters seemingly indifferent. The
highest service demands the greatest sacrifice, but it secures the
fullest blessing. But God claimed the right of determining the
personal appearance of His servant, and ordains that during all
the days of his separation no razor shall come upon his head. To
many minds there is the greatest shrinking from appearing
peculiar; but God would often have His people unmistakably
peculiar. Shall we not gladly render to Him all we are and have –
every member of our body, every fibre of our being, every faculty
of our mind, and will, and all our love?

24th Day

According to His Service

And the LORD spake unto Moses, saying, Take it of them
... and thou shalt give them unto the Levites, to every
man according to his service (Numbers 7:4, 5).

The princes brought their offering to the Lord, and the Lord
accepted it. Having accepted it, He chose to give it to the Levites,
for they in a special manner were His, and devoted to His service.

But the Lord did not say, divide it equally among the families
of Levi. There were six wagons, and three families of Levites;
but four wagons were given to Merari, two to Gershon, 'but
unto the sons of Kohath He gave none'. At first sight this seems
unfair; but it was and still is the Lord's plan to give 'to every
man according to his service'. It fell to the lot of Merari to carry
the heaviest materials of the tabernacle; the boards, the bars, and
the pillars with their heavy sockets of solid silver – the hundred
sockets alone weighed over five tons of silver – and all the
instruments, etc. – these formed Merari's weighty burden. The
duty of Gershon was to carry the curtains, hangings, coverings
and cords, etc., and for this service two wagons were as sufficient
help as the four for Merari. But what of Kohath? His burdens
were not light: the ark, with its covering the mercy-seat, and the
cherubim of gold overshadowing it, the table and the candlestick,
the altar and the vessels of the sanctuary, these were entrusted to
his sons. Heavy they were indeed, but no help had they, 'because
the service of the sanctuary belonging unto them was that they
should bear upon their shoulders.'

Sometimes the children of God are tempted to murmur when
their service seems heavy but little help is forthcoming: they may
perhaps compare their lot with others for whom larger provision
has been made. But God makes no mistakes; according to their
service He divides the help, and those that are called to the holiest
service are those who can have least assistance. Such are
privileged to carry upon their own shoulders sacred burdens that
may not be shared.

And he that offered his offering the first day was Nahshon the son of Amminadab, of the tribe of Judah (Numbers 7:12-17).

In this passage we come to the offerings of the twelve princes; and we note that, valuable as they manifestly were, the offerer, whose love prompted the gifts, is made more prominent in the inspired Record. And when the enumeration of his gifts has been fully given, we are again reminded of the offerer himself. Could the divine love and satisfaction be more expressly brought out?

With this thought in view, let us read between the lines of the Record. And he that offered his offering – for a glad, free-will offering it was – was Nahshon. Then follow the details of his gift, all for the enjoyment and satisfaction of God alone. Twelve times is all this detail given – a most emphatic evidence that God is never wearied in noting the service of His people. But even this is not all, for we then read of the gifts for the dedication of the altar. 'This' – all this – 'was the dedication of the altar.'

In this glad summing up of the great aggregate value of the offerings, we not only get a further view of the divine complacency in the love-gifts of His people, and in the persons of the offerers, but the object of the offerings is brought into special prominence. This was the dedication of the altar.

The importance of the brazen altar can scarcely be exaggerated. Apart from the brazen altar, there was no access for guilty man to the Tabernacle and all that it contained. Without shedding of blood there is no remission of sin.

Here then we see a marvellous revelation of divine love. First, an unrestricted invitation to draw near to God; woman or man, of any tribe – whosoever will – may come, but only in God's way. May God make our meditations very practical. Are we thus living? What conclusions do our brothers, sisters, children, friends, draw from our lives? Our givings for Christ's cause practically show our real estimate of the Cross.

The Divine Husbandman's Methods

> Every branch in Me that beareth not fruit He taketh away;
> and every branch that beareth fruit, He purgeth it,
> that it may bring forth more fruit (John 15:2).

To no prentice hand is committed the culture of the true Vine; the great Father Himself undertakes this; there is no under-husbandman. Speaking of Christ's people as a flock, under-shepherds are found; but as a branch each believer is directly united to the true Vine, which receives all things needful through the care of the great Husbandman Himself. This is very blessed; over-pruning or under-pruning is impossible: He will train and sustain every individual branch; the needs of each are known to Him and He will supply sunshine or shade, darkness or light, fair weather or shower, as seems best to Him. The branch may abide satisfied without care or worry.

We learn from these solemn words that it is possible to be in Christ and yet to bear no fruit. These words do not refer to mere professors, who are not really in Christ at all. The subject of this chapter is not salvation, but fruitfulness. The unfruitful branch taken away does not mean a soul lost, but a life lost. Men may be saved so as by fire, saved as Lot was saved out of Sodom; property gone, wife and children gone; saved, with a loss the extent of which eternity alone will reveal. The Lord keep His people from loving the world or the things of the world.

Not only does the great Husbandman remove the fruitless branches, but he purges the fruitful ones, that they may bring forth more fruit. The word rendered 'purgeth' is the verbal form of that rendered 'clean' in the next verse. The methods of the Divine Husbandman are not necessarily severe. He cleanses by the application of the Word; and where the gentle voice of the Spirit through the Word is listened to, severe and painful discipline may be unneeded. How much of restraint as well as of constraint we might be spared, did the Word of God dwell in us more richly, and were the leadings of the Spirit more implicitly obeyed!

Abiding in Christ

> Abide in Me, and I in you. As the branch cannot bear
> fruit of itself, except it abide in the vine;
> no more can ye, except ye abide in Me (John 15:4).

The word 'abide' simply means abide; it is also rendered in this chapter 'remain' and 'continue', and elsewhere is translated 'dwell'. The idea is rather that of rest than labour; it suggests not attainment or struggle, but quiescent enjoyment. Failure to recognize this simple fact lies at the root of many of the fallacies which hinder Christian people from enjoying the rest of God, abiding in Christ.

For years we ourselves longed to abide, but we thought of it as a very high attainment to which we were unequal; as involving spiritual heights to scale which we had not the needful strength; or a holding-on to which our weak powers were inadequate. Again, we confused abiding with feeding; we thought that abiding in Christ involved our fixing our mind upon Him, so as to retain at least the consciousness of His presence, however we might be occupied; failing in this we became utterly discouraged and bewildered. It could not be impossible to abide; and yet it seemed impossible to us, until we saw that what we thought of as abiding was rather feeding, which is a conscious and voluntary act. We partake of our food at stated intervals only, but we live and work in the strength of the food continuously. We had thought of abiding as struggling effort which required much strength, whereas abiding required no strength at all; none can be too weak to abide. Place a babe a month old in a cradle, and it will surely abide there; a year later it may not do so, getting an ugly fall in consequence.

Again, abiding is not a thing of consciousness, but of fact. Do we cease to abide in our homes when asleep at night? Or is our progress brought to an end if we fall asleep in the train? So abiding in Christ is not a thing of feeling or consciousness; it is a state which faith recognizes, and the reality of which is proved by its results.

How to Abide in Christ

Abide in Me, and I in you (John 15:4).

This double form of expression is peculiar and important. Our Saviour intended us to grasp the idea of a *mutual indwelling*, and He urges the maintenance of this condition. The double form conveys union and identification, as when a glass of wine and water are mingled.

We have not to learn how to *become* branches: 'Ye *are* the branches'. We did not become believers by struggling, but by trusting. How then shall we abide so as to secure, practically, all the blessings connected with this state? Let us consider what natural food effects for the natural body. Now while it does not impart life, it is essential to growth and development in the young, and in the adult to the sustaining of health and vigour. The whole body is indeed food transformed under the influence of life; and thus as we live in the body, from one point of view we may be said to abide in that which was our food. From another point of view we may say that our food abides in us. Thus we have a beautiful illustration of mutual abiding. So feeding upon Christ, we abide in Him, and He abides in us: 'He that eateth My flesh and drinketh My blood, dwelleth in Me, and I in him'.

Let us note the tense of the word 'eateth'. It is the habitual present. It is not said that to eat is to abide! But it is said that those who can and do feed are abiding. Many fail to abide because they habitually fast instead of feed. When once the babe has been built up into the man it is not possible to pick the man to pieces and reproduce the babe; but a slow process of starvation will soon leave a man as weak as a babe.

But some may say: 'I have habitually used the means of grace, but I have not been abiding, for I have not borne much fruit'. This is a common experience. A friend may slip a piece of gold into a poor man's pocket, but unless he find it he may pass the baker's shop and long for bread. When he discovers the money everything is changed. So, when the fact of abiding is recognized, joy is the immediate result. Faith must first grasp the fact.

1. The Will of God

Be not conformed to this world; but be ye transformed by the
renewing of your mind, that ye may prove what is that good,
and acceptable, and perfect Will of God (Romans 12:2).

The very fact that God is God should be sufficient to satisfy us
that His will is necessarily good and perfect, and to make it
acceptable to us. If infinite Love, possessed of unbounded resources
and infinite wisdom, wills anything, how can that Will be other
than good and perfect? And if it be not acceptable to us, does it
not clearly show that we are wrong and foolish? Our position as
true and loving children, redeemed at infinite cost by the mercies
of God, should surely constrain us to present our bodies unto
God as living sacrifices, and practically to lay our *all* upon the
altar for His service, seeking only to know and to do His will.

The passage before us indicates very clearly that there is a
Will of the World opposed to the Will of God. Each one of us
needs, with watchful care, to avoid conformity to the World's
will, and to seek that spiritual transformation which will bring
us into accordance with the Will of God. Theoretically, all
Christians will agree with this; but practically, it is often
overlooked, or insufficiently recognized.

It is an unlovely thing to see children greedily desiring to
obtain all they may from their parents, but caring little to show
that loving consideration and sympathy which a true parent's
heart must long for. But are we, as the children of God, sufficiently
careful to avoid this evil? May not an unrecognized selfishness
enter into our holy things, and even the Deepening of Spiritual Life
be sought rather from a desire to increase our spiritual enjoyment
than to be more acceptable to God or useful to our fellowmen?

If to be godly means to be Godlike; if to be true Christians
means to be Christlike; if to be holy means to be conformed to
the Holy Spirit of Promise, then surely we shall not be coveting
the highest, but prepared to take the lowest place, if thereby we
may bring salvation to the lost and ruined, wherever they may be.

2. The Will of God

Who gave Himself for our sins, that He might deliver us from this
present evil world, according to the Will of God and our Father
(Galatians 1:4).

The will and purpose of God is strikingly brought before us in
the Scripture. Of our Lord Jesus Christ we read: 'Who gave
Himself for our sins, that He might deliver us from this present
evil world according to the Will of God.' This great purpose
was no afterthought brought in when Satan had marred God's
beautiful creation. Far away in the distant ages of a past eternity
the Father had one treasure – His well-beloved Son. We are
told of Him: 'The Lord possessed Me in the beginning of His
way,... I was daily His delight.'

To Him it was that the Father, when He created the world,
entrusted the carrying out of His glorious design; and in Him
He found One always ready to do His will. But long ere He
created man in His own image, foreseeing that His image would
be marred, He purposed in His own will the redemption of the
fallen race. Oh, how great was the ransom! That loved One must
be given up. At such a price did God fulfil His own will. 'God
so loved the world, that He gave.'

And then the Son of God – the object of the Father's love – how
did He view this will of God? Did He empty Himself as of constraint?
Nay! He, 'for the joy that was set before Him, endured the cross,
despising the shame'. He laid down His life a willing sacrifice.

Ah, how little have we entered into the spirit of the Father and
of the Son! What unfaithful servants we have been! Glad to be
saved at the cost of a Saviour's life, how little have we been
prepared to give up our lives for His service. Is there any one of
us who is free from blood-guiltiness with regard to a perishing
world? It is possible to sing: 'My all is on the Altar', and yet be
unprepared to sacrifice a ring from one's finger, for the salvation
of the heathen. Where is that transforming, that renewing, of our
minds that makes our bodies really living sacrifices?

PART 2

THE LEGACY OF HIS LIFE

The second book which I wrote (and the first which I began) was that called *The Saints' Everlasting Rest*.... This book it pleased God so far to bless to the profit of many that it encouraged me to be guilty of all those scripts which after followed.... And I found that the transcript of the heart hath the greatest force on the hearts of others – Richard Baxter.

THE LEGACY OF HIS LIFE

Remember them ... considering the issue of their manner of life
(Hebrews 13:7, R.V. marg.).

We have considered the legacy of Hudson Taylor's message. To
speak of the legacy of his life as something apart may evoke
surprise. Should they not be one and the same? In the Perfect
Life the Word was made Flesh and dwelt among us. The Message
and the Life were one. Yet even with Christ the teaching expounds
the Life, and the Life personifies the teaching. The two are
necessary for a complete presentation. The prism does not add
anything to light, but only resolves it into its component colours.
How wondrously the unexpected and the unrealized glories of the
sun are revealed in the rainbow. So it is with the life and the message.

'It is well to remind ourselves', wrote Mr. Hudson Taylor, 'of
the close connection that exists between the written Word of God
and the incarnate Word of God. We shall never enjoy the one
apart from the other. It is through God's own revelation in the
written Word that we really see and know the Word who was
made flesh, and who rose from the dead.' Thus is revealed to us
the manifold, the many-coloured ($\pi o\lambda v\pi o\iota\kappa\iota\lambda o\varsigma$) wisdom and
grace of God.

On the other hand, a finished life cannot but speak with an
emphasis impossible to the spoken message. The whole is then
seen as distinct from its parts. The ruling passion becomes more
obvious. 'Let us see if his words be true, and let us try what
shall befall in the ending of his life', is a word recorded in *The
Wisdom of Solomon*. And it is interesting to note that the word
here translated 'ending' is the very one employed by the writer
of the Epistle to the Hebrews when he speaks of the 'issue' of
their lives. The word comes from a verb meaning 'to disembark'.
The voyage of life is finished; what is the 'outcome' of it all?
'Consider the issue of their manner of life,' says the inspired writer.
'Look it up and down' is Dr. Handley Moule's translation of the

verb. And Bishop Westcott renders it: 'Consider with attentive survey again and again.' The outcome of such lives is to be carefully scrutinized with the practical object of imitating their faith. We commemorate that we may aspire and endeavour.

In an orchestra each instrument has its own distinctive contribution. Not only is its note determined by the score, but its nature decides the quality of its tone and function. The flute can soothe, and the trumpet can stir, even when these two instruments are playing the same tune. The lower and the higher harmonics of the wood and the metal respectively, probably unrecognized, play their part in the whole effect. They give us the note and the timbre combined. And so it is in God's great orchestra. God's instruments differ. Each life may have not only its own distinctive message, but also its characteristic quality. We can see this in such lives as Luther's and Wesley's, or Bunyan's and Hudson Taylor's. The men and their dominant messages vary.

'The legacy which Bunyan has left us', writes Dr. Fullerton, 'is the assurance of grace. Grace! Grace abounding! Grace abounding to the chief of sinners! Not only is this the overwhelming subject of his great book, it is the one line upon which all his experience is threaded and the one theme to which he inevitably returns, no matter where he begins. In spite of the wonderful variety of his writings he is almost like Paganini playing on one string.'

With the alteration of one word only this passage might have been written of Hudson Taylor. Substitute 'faith' for 'grace' and not another change is necessary. The legacy Hudson Taylor has left us is the assurance of faith. Faith! Faith in God! Hold the faithfulness of God! Though we deny Him, yet He abideth faithful. This was the dominant message of his life, like the recurrent theme of a fugue. Though his contribution to the Christian Church is rich and varied, this is its outstanding feature. Faith in God was the strength of his life, and the explanation of his achievements.

That God would be faithful to His Word was to him so unquestionable a truth that he risked his all upon it, from his days as a medical student in Hull and London to the end of his years in China. It calls for some imagination today to realize how absolutely he staked his all on this belief. He chose no easy path; he faced the naked facts of life in their sternest and most unrelenting form. The world can be hard anywhere, but in a land where the love of God was unknown it could be peculiarly heartless and cruel. Yet he went where human succour was least likely. He burned his boats behind him, he ran every human risk, and he found faith to be substance, 'the substance of things hoped for, the evidence of things not seen'.

Consider his 'manner of life'. The word here used means more than life. In the Authorized Version it is translated 'conversation'. It means conduct, behaviour, walk, the daily converse, the goings up and down of life. Hudson Taylor's life was full of extraordinary vicissitudes and these made him conversant with men and affairs. Amid them all he proved the faithfulness of God. His long and varied career, with all its consequences, its issues, are a legacy to God's people. He has made it easier for those who follow him to trust God, to believe God, and to believe in God's promises. This is no small bequest.

We have ventured a comparison between the legacy of Bunyan and the legacy of Hudson Taylor, between Grace and Faith. Yet each truth had the same source and end – God. 'I was never out of the Bible,' said Bunyan; nor was Hudson Taylor. 'If I should now venture all for God, I engage God to take care of my concernments.' The words are Bunyan's, but they might be Hudson Taylor's. 'I could not be content with saying I believe and am sure; methought I was more than sure (if it is lawful so to express myself) that these things which I asserted were true.' This is the confidence of the author of *Grace Abounding*. But let us hear Hudson Taylor: 'Faith, I now see,' he writes, 'is "the *substance* of things hoped for", and not mere shadows. It is not less than sight, but *more*. Sight only shows the outward form of things; faith gives the substance. You can *rest* on substance, *feed* on substance.'

Bunyan, when faced with the gallows, could still say: 'I am

for going on, and venturing my eternal state with Christ, whether I have comfort or not. I will leap off the ladder, even blindfold, into eternity, sink or swim, come heaven, come hell. Lord Jesus, if Thou wilt catch me, do; if not, I will venture for Thy Name.' When any man is thus prepared to give his life for a principle, his words and his testimony take on a new value. 'What erewhile bore the image and superscription of Caesar seems now to bear the image and superscription of God.' All Hudson Taylor's utterances were stamped with these credentials. His own life proved the stress he laid upon the authority of God, God's authority to command, His authority to open and to shut, and His control over winds and waves. He believed that heaven and earth might pass away, but not God's Word. God, to him, was 'not a man that He should lie, neither the son of man, that He should repent. Hath he said, and shall He not do it? Or hath He spoken, and shall He not make it good? was his assured conviction. He believed that Christ's assertion, 'All authority hath been given unto Me in heaven and on earth', was no fine yet empty phrase, but a glorious fact on which to build. Like Bunyan he was prepared to venture all for the Name.

It was the life, dominated by this faith, which gave his messages their power. It is the person behind the word that gives it authority. The faith of the Philippian gaoler began by faith in Paul and Silas as men. Their manner of life in prison and in the earthquake begat conviction. 'It was no ordinary expression of politeness, but something much liker worship, when he, the gaoler, called his two prisoners κυριοι.'[1] It is the same always. It is the life that authenticates the message. And the messages explain the life.

We had originally intended to group under this heading some of those messages which were, in a special sense, associated with Hudson Taylor's life, but it has proved practically impossible to draw any hard and fast line between the reading appropriate for this and the other sections. He had no creed apart from life.

---

1. Translated *Sirs*, but meaning *Lords* and *Masters*.

Hold God's Faithfulness

Such we believe to be the purport of the three words of our Lord that in our version of Mark 11:22, are rendered: 'Have faith in God', and in the margin more literally, 'Have the faith of God'.[1]

Man needs a creed, and will have one. Here is an inspired creed: short, intelligible and to the point. It meets every man's need, is suitable to every age and to every country, and appropriate in every circumstance of daily life. It bears on all man's temporal affairs, it meets his every spiritual want. To God's faithfulness should we look for our necessary food – 'Give us this day our daily bread.' To Him, too, should we look for raiment, for He clothes the lilies of the field. Every care for temporal things we should bring to Him, and then be careful for nothing. To Him likewise should we come with all spiritual want, 'that we may obtain mercy, and find grace to help in time of need'. Is our path dark? He is our sun. Are we in danger? He is our shield. If we trust Him, we shall not be put to shame; but if our faith fail, His will not – 'If we believe not, He abideth faithful'.

Want of trust is at the root of almost all our sins and all our weaknesses; and how shall we escape from it, but by looking to Him, and observing His faithfulness? As the light which shines from the dark waters of the lake is the reflection of the sun's rays, so man's faith is the impress and reflection of God's faith. The man who holds God's faith will not be reckless or foolhardy, but he will be ready for every emergency. The man who holds God's faith will dare to obey Him, however impolitic it may appear.

---

1. For the rendering 'God's faithfulness', see Romans 3:3, where 'the faith of God' evidently means His faithfulness. The verb translated 'hold' is similarly rendered in Matthew 21:26, 'All *hold* John as a prophet'. In the corresponding passage in Mark 11:32, it is rendered 'count'; and in that in Luke 20:6, a different Greek word is used, which well illustrates the meaning, 'They be *persuaded* that John was a prophet'. Let us see that in theory we *hold* that God is faithful; that in daily life we *count* upon it; and that at all times and under all circumstances we are fully *persuaded* of this blessed truth.

2nd Day

Have Faith in God

And Jesus answering, saith unto them, Have faith in God
(Mark 11:22).

Hold God's faithfulness. Abraham held God's faith, and offered up Isaac, accounting that God was able to raise him up. Moses held God's faith, and led the millions of Israel into the waste howling wilderness. Joshua knew Israel well, and was ignorant neither of the fortification of the Canaanites, nor of their martial prowess: but he held God's faithfulness, and led Israel across Jordan. The Apostles held God's faith, and were not daunted by the hatred of the Jews, nor by the hostility of the heathen. And what shall I say more, for the time would fail me to tell 'of those who, holding God's faithfulness, had faith, and by it subdued kingdoms, wrought righteousness, obtained promises, stopped the mouths of lions, quenched the violence of fire, escaped the edge of the sword, out of weakness were made strong, waxed valiant in fight, turned to flight the armies of aliens'.

Satan, too, has his creed: 'Doubt God's faithfulness'. 'Hath God said? Are you not mistaken as to His commands? He could not really mean so. You take an extreme view – give too literal a meaning to the words.' Ah! how constantly, and alas, how successfully, are such arguments used to prevent whole-hearted trust in God, whole-hearted consecration to God.

All God's giants have been weak men, who did great things for God because they reckoned on God being with them. See the cases of David, of Jonathan and his armour-bearer, of Asa, Jehoshaphat and many others. Oh! beloved friends, if there is a living God, faithful and true, let us hold His faithfulness. Holding His faithfulness, we may face, with calm and sober but confident assurance of victory, every difficulty and danger. We may count on grace for the work, on pecuniary aid, on needful facilities, and on ultimate success. Let us not give Him a partial trust, but daily, hourly, serve Him, 'holding God's faithfulness'.

The Words denoting 'Faith'

In support of Mr. Taylor's translation of 'Have faith in God', now become one of the Watchwords of the China Inland Mission, it may be helpful to quote a few lines from Bishop Lightfoot's scholarly study of the word 'Faith' in his Commentary on *Galatians*, pp. 152-162.

The Greek πιστις, the Latin *fides*, and the English 'faith', hover between two meanings; *trustfulness*, the frame of mind which relies upon another; and *trustworthiness* the frame of mind which can be relied upon. Not only are the two connected together grammatically, as active and passive senses of the same word, or logically, as subject and object of the same act; but there is a close moral affinity between them. Fidelity, constancy, firmness, confidence, reliance, trust, belief – there are the links which connect the two extremes, the passive with the active meaning of 'faith' ....

The history of the term for 'faith', in the three sacred languages of Christian theology is instructive from more points of view than one....

1. There is in Biblical Hebrew no corresponding substantive for 'faith', the active principle. Its nearest representative is... 'firmness, constancy, trustworthiness'....

2. Unlike the Hebrew, the Greek word seems to have started from an active meaning.... In the Old Testament, there being no equivalent to the active meaning, πιστις has always the passive sense, 'fidelity', 'constancy'.... In the New Testament πιστις is found in both its passive and active sense. On the other hand it is used for constancy, trustworthiness, whether of the immutable purpose of God, Romans 3:3, or of good faith, honesty, uprightness in men, Matthew 23:23.... On the other hand, as 'faith', 'belief', it assumes in the teaching of our Lord, enforced and explained by St. Paul, the foremost place in the phraseology of Christian doctrine....

3. It has been seen that the meaning of the Greek πιστις was reflected on its Hebrew original. Not less was this meaning infused into its Latin rendering. The verb πιστευω was naturally translated by *credo*, but this root supplied no substantive corresponding to πιστις, no adjective (for *credulus* was stamped with a bad meaning)

corresponding to πιστος. Words were therefore borrowed from another source, *fides*, *fidelis*.... Its introduction into Christian literature at length stamped it with a new image and superscription.

4. The English terms 'faith' and 'faithful', derived from the Latin *fides*, have inherited the latitude of meaning which marked their ancestry.

3rd Day

Self-denial versus Self-assertion

If any man would come after Me, let him deny himself, and take up his cross daily, and follow Me (Luke 9:23).

We might naturally have thought that if there is one thing in the life of the Lord Jesus Christ which belongeth to Him alone, it was His cross-bearing. To guard against so natural a mistake the Lord Jesus teaches us that if any man will be His disciple he *must* – not he may – deny himself, and take up his cross and follow his Lord. Is there not a needs-be for this exhortation? Are not self-indulgence and self-assertion temptations to which we are ever exposed and to which we constantly give way without even a thought of the un-Christliness of such conduct? Self-denial surely means something far greater than some slight and insignificant lessening of self-indulgence!

As believers, we claim to have been crucified together with Christ; and Paul understood this, not imputatively but practically. He does not say, I take up my cross daily, in the light, modern sense of the expression; he puts it rather as dying daily; and therefore, as one 'in deaths oft', he was never surprised, or stumbled, by any hardship or danger involved in his work.

We wish, however, to draw attention to another aspect of self-denial which is often overlooked. What does the Word of God teach us about our rights, our claims, our dues? What did our Saviour intend to teach us by the parable of Matthew 18:23-35; 'Ought you not to have mercy on your fellow-servant, as I had on you?' Can that slave, under these circumstances, assert and claim his right over his fellow.

Is not this principle of non-assertion, of this aspect of self-denial, a far-reaching one? Did our Lord claim His right before Pilate's bar, and assert Himself; or did His self-denial and cross-bearing go the length of waiting for His Father's vindication? And shall we be jealous of our own honour and rights, as men and as citizens of Western countries, when what our Master wants is witness to and reflection of His own character and earthly life?

71

Hereunto were ye Called

If, when ye do well, and suffer for it, ye shall take it patiently,
this is acceptable with God. For hereunto were ye called
(1 Peter 2:20-21).

The Christian calling is as unintelligible and as unattractive to
unbelief as was the person and work of our glorious Head. In
the world's judgment He had no form or comeliness, no beauty
that they should desire Him. It is possible to receive salvation
and eternal life through Christ, but with a very imperfect
appreciation of the nature, the privileges, and the responsibilities
of our calling. To what then are we called? *To do well, to suffer
for it, and to take it patiently.* 'A pretty calling,' says Unbelief,
and turns away in disgust. 'Sad, but true,' responds many a true
but sad heart. 'I thank Thee, O Father,' says Strong Faith, 'for
so it seemed good in Thy sight.' God has not changed since the
Holy Spirit recorded the answer to the question given above.
Man has not changed; nor has the great enemy of souls changed.

Now, none of the proceedings of God are arbitrary: all the
acts and all the requirements of perfect wisdom and of perfect
goodness must of necessity be wise and good. We are called when
we so suffer to take it patiently – and more than patiently, thankfully
and joyfully – because seen from a right point of view there is
neither ground nor excuse for impatience, but on the contrary
abundant cause for overflowing thanks and joy. The early
Christians were neither fools nor madmen when they took joyfully
the spoiling of their goods, exulting that their names were cast
out as evil, and that they themselves were counted worthy to suffer.

To make the message intelligible, it must be *lived*. God says,
in effect: 'Go and live among these unconverted ones as my
representative.' Be really glad, and let them see that you are glad
– at the cost of any personal wrong and suffering – to have an
opportunity of making the grace of God intelligible. The greater
the persecutions are, the greater the power of your testimony.
Such testimony never was in vain.

More Blessed to Give

Remember the words of the Lord Jesus, how He Himself said,
It is more blessed to give than to receive (Acts 20:35).

Oh, that our pen may be anointed as with fresh oil, while we seek
to bring our own soul, and the soul of our readers, more fully
under the influence of this truth!

Our gracious Lord did not content Himself with merely giving
utterance to this truth; He embodied it in life. He exhibited it in
death. He emptied Himself that we might be filled. He gave – ah!
what did He not give? – He gave Himself for us. Oh, for hearts
to apprehend and live this out!

Why is our fulness in Christ so little experienced? Why is it
not more enjoyed? Simply because we fail to give freely. How
little does the Church realize how she is *impoverishing* herself,
while she is to an awfully large extent leaving the world to perish
through her unbelief, her selfishness, her parsimony. What does
her life say to the world? Christ has given her light; she denies it
to the perishing. Christ has said, 'to *every* creature'; the Church
says, 'No, No, No! At home to some extent, if you like; but
abroad – No. A few missionaries, if you like; but many – No.
Will I impoverish myself for the sake of the perishing? No.'

We rejoice to know that there are many who believe that it *is*
more blessed to give than to receive; but we unhesitatingly affirm
that the general testimony given by the professing Church, as a
whole, to the unbelieving world at large is that it is *not* more
blessed to give than to receive. No wonder scepticism increases
and infidelity prospers!

Whether we believe it or no, 'it *is* more blessed to give than
to receive'. If we will but be givers, He will minister to us both
seed for our sowing and bread for our eating, and we shall always
have all sufficiency in all things, and abound in all good works.
Only become givers, and it is immaterial whether you have five
loaves or five hundred; the larger number would no more suffice,
apart from Divine and multiplying power, than the smaller.

> Abide in Me, and I in you. As the branch cannot bear
> fruit of itself, except it abide in the vine; so neither
> can ye, except ye abide in Me (John 15:4).

We need not enlarge upon the importance of abiding in Christ. If we do *not* abide in Him, it is not that we bear less fruit or inferior fruit, but apart from Him we can do *nothing*. It is either fruit and abiding, or no fruit at all, nothing but mere works. The distinction between fruit and works is important. Works do not show the character of the worker, but only his skill: a bad man may make a good chair. Works, again, may be good and useful, but do not propagate themselves. Fruit on the contrary, reveals the character of the fruit-bearer, and has its seed in itself – is productive.

What is the meaning of the words: 'Abide in Me and I in you'? The two words, 'I AM', are the key to this chapter. The question is not what *you* are, not what *you* can do. '*I Am* the true Vine,' and further, '*My Father* is the Husbandman.' He turns our thoughts away from self altogether, and practically says, 'Believe in God, believe also in Me'.

'I am the Vine.' Not any part of the Vine, but the whole Vine. The vine is the whole tree – root, trunk, branches, twigs, leaves, flowers, fruit. Some of us, failing to see this, have read the passage as though it were written, 'I am the Root: ye are the branches'; and we have said, 'Ah! there is fatness enough in the Root, and how am I to get the rich sap into my poor, puny branch?' The branch gets nothing *out* of the vine, it enjoys all *in* the vine. So are we *in* Christ. The little word 'in' requires more than a passing notice. It is not in the sense of within, as when the less is contained within the greater. As used in the text, *in* implies *union with*, identification. The branch is vitally and organically one with the vine, as the eye or ear is *in* the body. And the word *abide* conveys the idea of rest, rather than of labour or motion, of enjoyment attained, not of seeking and striving.

The twofold expression indicates a mutual indwelling. Recognise both truths, not sometimes, but at all times.

74

How to Abide in Christ

> I am the Vine, ye are the branches: He that abideth in Me,
> and I in him, the same beareth much fruit: for apart
> from Me ye can do nothing (John 15:5).

There is only one way in which this can possibly be done – *by faith*. We are saved by faith, and we live by faith. But we must not be occupied about our faith, but about the object of faith. Not with the law of optics, nor with the construction of the eye, must we be occupied, if we would enjoy a beautiful landscape; we must look at it and feast upon it. So we must not be looking inward and considering the nature and extent of our faith, but must look out, and be occupied with the Promiser and with His promises.

Accept by faith the statements of Scripture on the subject of abiding in all their fulness. Christ not only uses the present tense in saying: 'I am the Vine', but also in 'Ye *are* the branches'. His word is not Seek, Strive, but Count on what I am, and on what is *now* your relation to Me. Some may say, 'I do not find the fruit of abiding'. This undoubtedly will be true if we have not claimed by faith the fulfilment of God's promises. God gave Canaan to Israel by promise, yet they had to obtain the promise. Wherever they set down their foot, wherever they drove out their foes, claiming fearlessly their possession, they obtained it. So shall we. Do not, however, go beyond the Word. We are nowhere taught that abiding in Christ implies sinlessness. On the other hand, if abiding is not sinlessness, neither is it compatible with indulgence in any known sin. 'These things write I unto you that ye sin not.'

In conclusion. Our union with Christ is a precious truth. It is a fact, not a feeling. A man is as much one with his wife when asleep as when awake, when abroad as when at home. Consciousness and enjoyment may spring from it, but neither constitute it nor contribute towards it. It is independent of both. From the consciousness of union springs the power to abide. Let us then – not seek, nor wait – but now accept by faith the Saviour's word – 'Ye *are* the branches'.

These things have I spoken unto you, that My joy might remain in you, and that your joy might be full (John 15:11).

I have lately been visiting our stations in the Chekiang province, and the beautiful scenery has vividly reminded me of the time when I was your guest in Switzerland. The hills here, of course, are not so high, and there are no glacier views; but they are very fine, and the almost tropical beauty and fertility compensate for some drawbacks. When you are tired of European scenery, you must come and see ours! But alas! in this beautiful land no one heeds the Maker of it all.

Except a few sheet-tracts posted in front of some rest-sheds and temples by some of our own Chinese workers I did not see or hear for days of any witness for the Lord. All is of earth, earthy indeed. When will even the passing evangelist reach the hundredth part of China's villages and towns with his message?

At each station I have lately visited I have been introduced to Christians converted since my previous visit, and in many places there is promise of a coming harvest. Our great need is for more spiritual power in those now in the field – missionaries and Chinese workers – of more Chinese Christians filled with the Spirit, living for Christ alone; and of more foreign missionaries to lead the way.

There are plenty willing to hear, but few fitted for speaking of Christ as a 'living, bright reality', from the overflow of a heart full of *unintermitting* joy in the Lord. Yet this surely is our portion, and our duty. There is no such thing in *nature* as an intermitting communication of life – as from the vine to the branch, from the body to the members. Should there be in grace?

Does not Christ give us His peace, His joy – Himself – to be our *constant* life and peace and joy and power? 'In Thy name shall they rejoice all the day.' 'They shall walk, O Lord, in the light of Thy countenance.'

---

1. From a personal letter.

A Full Trust

Be careful for nothing; but in everything, by prayer and supplication, with thanksgiving, let your requests be made known unto God. And the peace of God, which passeth all understanding, shall keep your hearts and minds through Christ Jesus (Philippians 4:6, 7).

Familiar, precious words to every child of God! We love to ponder them. We have doubtless often tried to carry out the command, and may have prayed earnestly and frequently to be enabled to do so. And yet are we not conscious that we are not careful for nothing, and that the peace of God does not always keep our hearts and minds? We have much peace, perhaps, but it is not unbroken.

What is the powerful, though unspoken, testimony of our lives and hearts about this word of command, which, like every other, calls not for admiration merely, but for full, and complete, and constant obedience? We have prayed to obey, and failed; and now we are practically saying that this is a hard saying – beautiful indeed as an ideal, but in ordinary life impracticable.

Then comes the question: Why have we failed? Is it not because, though asking God to help us, we have been trying to do our part? And 'our part' is sure to be attended with failure. We have heard it said that 'God's commandings are enablings', but we have not realized that *only* from the God who commands can the power come to obey.

What the rest and relief are of having the last atom of care lifted from the spirit none can know but those who have experienced it. Nor is this some high attainment. Was it an attainment when we first came to Jesus in utter helplessness, and casting ourselves at His feet found in Him pardon and peace? Was it not all free grace? Will you not come again as you came then, that as His grace then saved you from the consequences of your sins, so now it may save you from their power?

God Only

My soul, wait thou only upon God; for my expectation is
from Him. He only is my Rock and my Salvation: He is my
defence; I shall not be moved (Psalm 62:5, 6).

To most of God's children there come times of sudden
awakening when some unexpected trial, an illness, or a
bereavement has revealed to us, with startling effect, how, all
unconsciously perhaps, our souls were not waiting 'only upon
God', but were leaning on an instrument, or on circumstances.
Our expectation was from our own effort, or from some chosen
leader. And as it was not entirely 'from Him', we are moved,
perhaps almost crushed. In the trial our impulse is to turn to
man; but the help of man may be unavailing – perhaps even his
sympathy we cannot count on. We have *only* God to go to; and
so we are driven to fall back upon Him. But surely, surely, He
should not be our last resource; rather the first to whom we turn
in our difficulties whether they be small or great.

Alas, how often, if the true secret were discovered, might it
be found that God's power was *stayed*, because He would not
give His glory to another. Man's power, what is it? We wrestle
not against flesh and blood; how then can an arm of flesh
overcome? Oh, let Christian workers beware lest in any degree
God's good gifts be trusted instead of Himself! 'When I am weak
then am I strong,' said the great Apostle; but how unpopular
among us his cause of glorying: 'Most gladly, therefore, will I
rather glory in my infirmity, that the power of Christ may rest
upon me. Therefore, I take pleasure in infirmities, in reproaches,
in necessities, in persecutions, in distresses for Christ's sake.'
And yet is *any* cost too great that the power of Christ may rest
upon us? One only Rock, one only Salvation, one only Defence
is ours, and just in proportion as anything else is substituted will
there be weakness, and failure, and sin. Power with God will be
the real gauge of power with men.

11th Day

Winning Christ

I count all things but loss for the excellency of the knowledge of Christ Jesus my Lord: for whom I have suffered the loss of all things, and do count them but dung, that I may win Christ (Philippians 3:8).

Do we give sufficient attention to the subject of winning Christ? It is our joy and privilege to know Him as God's unspeakable *gift*; but none knew this more fully than the Apostle Paul. But was he satisfied with this knowledge? Or was his soul-consuming desire, at all possible cost, to *win* Christ; and thus to know Him, and the power of His resurrection, and the fellowship of His sufferings? Oh that Christ may be so known by each one of us as a 'living, bright reality', that our one desire – our one absorbing heart-passion may be, that we may personally *win* Christ – may personally know Him as the Apostle longed to do.

What is meant by winning Christ? The meaning of the verb is to gain – by traffic or exchange. In the case of many a believer it may be truthfully said that Christ has a large place in his heart, though he could not perhaps fully say, Christ *is* all, *in* all; much that is gain to him has not yet become loss that he might win Christ. How may we win Christ? By gladly surrendering, on our part, that which naturally we should most value, in His service; and also by heartily acquiescing in each loss and each cross which a Father's love ordains.

We know that He does remove many a source of joy, and we know that He does reveal Himself through the removal more fully than ever before. But it is a triumph of faith which brings great glory to God when, in the time of nature's sorrow, the whole soul of the believer rejoicingly accepts the Lord's dealings. When flesh and heart fail, when our fondest hopes and desires are crossed, when it is quite clear to us that it is His will, not ours, that is being done, and our hearts are still enabled to rejoice in that will – then indeed do we *win* Christ; and oh, what a winning is that!

12th Day

A Word of Cheer

I will go before thee, and make the crooked places straight (Isaiah 45:2).

This message is a word of cheer from the Master Himself. 'I will go before thee, and make the crooked places straight.' This word has been a feast to my soul and a pillow for my head. It is just as fresh and prized today as it has been in the months that are passed – amongst difficulties that have each seemed in turn to be almost insurmountable.

Satan would have us try today to bear tomorrow's burden with only today's grace, and would dismay us with anticipation of trouble which looms in the distance, leading us to disobey the directions: 'Take no thought for the morrow'; 'Be careful for nothing'; but what a privilege it is to be permitted to rest upon the assurance: 'I will go before thee'; thou shalt not be without a Guide, and 'He that followeth Me shall not walk in darkness'. 'I will make the crooked places straight', the rugged places plain, and when thou comest up to them thou shalt find insurmountable difficulty already removed, that thy foes, like Jehoshaphat's, have slain themselves, that thou hast to strip off the spoils, and to make the valley one, not of conflict, but of praise – a Berachah.

Again and again it has been so in China, and doubtless many at home can bear the same testimony. A difficulty in the family which they were powerless to cope with, a perplexity in the profession or business, a spiritual difficulty, or one connected with service for the Lord, has threatened to disturb the peace and to fill with dismay, but it has been rolled upon the Lord, and given over to Him to manage or arrange; the command has been obeyed: 'In everything by prayer and supplication let your requests be made known unto God,' and the promised peace of God garrisoning the heart has kept the care and worry outside until the time came to find the trouble bereft of its sting, the crooked places made straight. Perhaps there are few who can look back without seeing that such cares as have been borne ought to have been dealt with and dismissed.

13th Day

God's Badge

> Bid them that they make fringes in the borders of their
> garments... and that they put upon the fringe of the borders a
> ribband of blue... that ye may look upon it and remember all
> the commandments of the LORD... (Numbers 15:38-39).

The ordinance concerning this 'ribband of blue' closes an important chapter. It commences with instructions concerning the burnt-offering; then concerning the first-fruits, and then concerning errors from heedlessness and ignorance. But occasion was taken in connection with the judgment of a case of presumptuous sin to introduce the wearing of the 'ribband of blue'.

God would have all His people wear a badge. They were to make them fringes in the borders of their garments, and to put upon the fringes a ribband of blue, that they might look upon it and remember all the commandments of the Lord, and do them, and might be a holy people. Blue is the colour of heaven. When the clouds come between, then, and only then, is the deep blue lost. It is the will of God that there should never be a cloud between His people and Himself, and that as the Israelite of old, wherever he went, carried the ribband of blue, so His people today should manifest a heavenly spirit and temper wherever they go, and should, like Moses, in their very countenances bear witness to the glory and beauty of the God whom they love and serve.

How interesting it must have been to see that ribband of blue carried by the farmer into the field, by the merchant to his place of business, by the maid-servant into the innermost parts of the dwelling, when performing her daily duties. Is it less important that the Christian of today, called to be a witness for Christ, should be manifestly characterised by His spirit? Should we not all be 'imitators of God, as dear children', and 'walk in love, as Christ also hath loved us, and given Himself for us'? And should not this spirit of God-likeness be carried into the smallest details of life, and not be merely reserved for special occasions?

Be ye therefore perfect, even as your Father
which is in heaven is perfect (Matthew 5:48).

We are to be the salt of the earth and the light of the world, not to break one of the least of the commandments, not to give way to anger, nor to tolerate the thought of impurity, to give no rash promises, or in conversation to say more than yea or nay. The spirit of retaliation is not to be indulged in; a yieldingness of spirit is to characterise the child of the Kingdom, and those who hate and despitefully use us are to be pitied, and loved, and prayed for.

In the little frictions of daily life, as well as in the more serious trials and persecutions to which the Christian is exposed, he is manifestly to be an imitator of his heavenly Father. Now, God's perfection is an absolute perfection, while ours, at best, is only relative. A needle may be a perfect needle, in every way adapted for its work: it is not a microscopic object; under the magnifying power it becomes a rough, honeycombed poker. So we are not called to be perfect angels, or in any respect divine, but we are to be perfect Christians, performing the privileged duties that as such devolve upon us.

Now our Father makes *according to His perfection* the least thing that He makes. The tiniest fly, the smallest animalcule, the dust of a butterfly's wing, however highly you may magnify them, are seen to be absolutely perfect. Should not the little things of daily life be as relatively perfect in the case of the Christian as lesser creations of God are perfect as His work? Ought we not to glorify God in the formation of each letter that we write, and to write a more legible hand as Christians than unconverted people can be expected to do? Ought we not to be more thorough in our service, not simply doing well that which will be seen and noticed, but, as our Father makes many a flower to bloom unseen in the lonely desert, so to do all that we can do as under His eye, though no other eye ever take note of it?

Divine Strength

My grace is sufficient for thee (2 Corinthians 12:9).

We can, some of us, look back to the time when we were afraid to make public confession of Christ from fear that we might not have strength to serve Him worthily. We forgot that we had not saved ourselves, and that while we could not keep ourselves, the Lord would be our Keeper. And are there not many of the Lord's people who are kept back from foreign service by feeling they have not sufficient grace. To all such we would give Christ's own word to His servant Paul: 'My grace is sufficient for thee'.

Few of the servants of God have had a more difficult and trying path than the Apostle. His one desire was 'to know Him, and the power of His resurrection' if by any means he might attain 'unto the resurrection of the dead'. We understand him to mean by this attainment not a share in the *general* resurrection nor even a share in the *first* resurrection. His thought we gather to be a *present* attainment of resurrection life and power, so that while in the world he would live practically as one who had died and been raised, and was above and beyond its influence. It involved, as he foresaw, his being perfected through sufferings.

To him the Lord Jesus was no mere abstraction. Again and again in times of special difficulty he had special revelations of the Lord Jesus, and having heard unspeakable words he was enabled to labour more abundantly, to bear imprisonments, and be in deaths oft. In all he was upheld by the present power of God. But the Lord in His grace – not in chastening for falls, but to keep him from that danger – suffered the messenger of Satan to buffet him. And when he besought the Lord thrice that this affliction might be taken away, his prayer was answered by the Lord Himself: 'My grace is sufficient for thee, for My power is made perfect in weakness'. Henceforth he *knew* himself to be in just the very position to be made a blessing to others. His prayer was not rejected, nor unanswered; and yet his request was not granted as he asked it.

God's Better Answer

My grace is sufficient for thee (2 Corinthians 12:9).

Do we not get, both in the case of the Lord Jesus and of the Apostle Paul, much light on the question so often asked: 'Does God always answer prayer?' There are, of course, many prayers that He does not answer – prayers that are asked amiss, that are contrary to God's revealed will, or that are unmixed with faith. But there are many other prayers that are proper petitions, offered in a proper spirit, in which nevertheless the answer does not come just in the way in which the offerer may have expected. When a great need is brought before God in prayer, He may answer that prayer by supplying the need or by removing it: just as we may balance a pair of scales by adding to the light scale, or reducing the weight in the other. Paul was distressed by a burden which he had not strength to bear, and asked that the burden might be removed. God answered the prayer, not by taking it away, but by showing him the power and the grace to bear it joyfully. Thus that which had been the cause of sorrow and regret now became the occasion of rejoicing and triumph.

And was not this really a better answer to Paul's prayer than the mere removing of the thorn? The latter course would have left him open to the same trouble when the next distress came; but God's method at once and for ever delivered him from all the oppression of the present and of all future similar trials. Hence he triumphantly exclaims: 'Most gladly therefore will I rather glory and rejoice in my weakness that the strength of Christ may overshadow and cover me'. Ah! who would not wish to share in the Apostle's thorn in the flesh, if thereby he might be brought in reality into the experience of his deliverance from the oppression of all weakness, all injury, all necessity, all persecution, all distress; and might henceforth know that the very hour and time of weakness was the hour and time of truest strength? Let none fear then to step out in glad obedience to the Master's commands.

The Result of Coming to the King

And King Solomon gave unto the Queen of Sheba all her
desire, whatsoever she asked, beside that which Solomon gave
her of his royal bounty (1 Kings 10:13).

If we learn from this narrative how to approach the anti-type of
King Solomon, and to receive from Him blessings as much
greater than those received by the Queen of Sheba as Christ is
greater than Solomon, we shall not meditate without profit on
this portion of Scripture.

In many respects we resemble the Queen of Sheba. Though
of royal birth, she was doubtless black, because the sun had
looked on her. The post she was called to occupy was no easy
one; in her own life, and in her duty towards others, she found
many hard questions. She heard of one who might afford her the
help she needed. And she came not empty-handed; she came not
only to receive but also to give. Her journey accomplished, she
was granted the audience her soul craved. She not only
unburdened her camels, she unburdened her own heart, and found
that her difficult questions were no difficulty to him. 'Solomon
told her all her questions; there was not anything hid from the
king which he told her not.' And so gracious was he that, without
restraint, 'she communed with him of *all* that was in her heart'.
Do we recognise the majesty of the King of glory, and the immortal
honour that appertains to His service? To those who do, the glad
exclamations of the Queen of Sheba afford well-suited
expressions: 'Happy are Thy subjects, happy are Thy servants,
which stand continually before Thee and hear Thy wisdom'.

Has Christ become to us such a living, bright reality that no
post of duty shall be irksome, that as His witnesses we can return to
the quiet home side, or to the distant service, with hearts more than
glad, more than satisfied, even it may be when stripped of earthly
friends and treasures? But King Solomon had to send the Queen
of Sheba away; he could not go with her. Our Solomon goes with
us, nay dwells in us. We have His word: 'I will never leave thee.'

A Full Reward

The LORD recompense thy work, and a full reward be given thee of
the LORD God of Israel, under whose wings thou art come to trust
(Ruth 2:12).

In this interesting narrative we have another instance of the way
in which the Holy Spirit teaches by typical lives. The coming of
the Queen of Sheba to Solomon taught us how hard questions
are to be solved and our hearts to be fully satisfied. Here we have
a still higher lesson: how to serve so as to obtain a full reward,
while as to the nature of that reward no little light is given us.

Ruth was by nature 'a stranger to the commonwealth of Israel',
but by marriage she was brought among that people. On the
death of her husband, she still clave to her mother-in-law, and to
her God. If companionship with one of God's poor servants is so
precious, what shall we say to Him who exhorts us: 'Go ... and
lo, I am with you alway'? We next find Ruth toiling in the sun as
a gleaner, and there she meets for the first time the lord of the
harvest. And poor Ruth, though not a reaper – only a gleaner – is
made most welcome, and encouraged to remain until all the
reaping is done. With touching simplicity and humility the grateful
gleaner replies: 'Why have I found grace in thine eyes, that thou
shouldest take knowledge of me?'

Let us turn from Boaz to the true Lord of the Harvest. Does
He meet *us* there, toiling in the heat of summer's sun? Knowing
fully *all* we have done, does that knowledge bring joy to His
heart? Let us all leave the fatherland of the world, or at least
become strangers and pilgrims in it. Where the need is greatest
let us be found gladly obeying the Master's command. For it is
in the harvest-field, it is among the reapers, that we shall find
Him. Happy toiler in China! If it is sometimes dark, the shadow
is but the shadow of His wings. And he who comforted and blessed
the lowly and lonely gleaner while the harvest lasted became her
husband when the harvest toil was past. It was *thus* the Lord
recompensed her work.

1. Blessed Prosperity

Blessed is the man that walketh not in the
counsel of the ungodly (Psalm 1:1).

There is a prosperity which is not blessed: it comes not from above but from beneath. This prosperity of the wicked is often a sore perplexity to the servants of God. Many beside the Psalmist have been tempted to ask: 'Is there knowledge in the Most High?' While Satan remains the god of this world, this source of perplexity will continue to those who do not enter the sanctuary and consider the latter end of the worldling.

But thank God there is a true prosperity which comes from Him and leads towards Him. It is not only consistent with perfect integrity and uncompromising holiness of heart and life, but it cannot be attained without them. This divine prosperity is God's purpose for every believer in *all* that he undertakes; in things temporal and in things spiritual. It is God's will for each child of His that 'whatsoever he doeth shall prosper'. Shall we not each ask: How is it with me? Is this blessed prosperity my experience? If it be not so, what is the reason?

The first characteristic given us is that the blessed man walks not in the counsel of the ungodly. Notice it does not say he walks not in wicked counsel. A man of God would not do that. It says: 'He walks not in the counsel of the wicked.' Now the wicked have often much worldly wisdom, but the child of God should be on his guard against their counsel. The Word of God will make him wiser than all such counsellors. And the wise child of God will carefully ascertain the standpoint of a fellow-believer, for Satan frequently makes handles of the people of God, as in Peter's case. Little did the astonished Peter know whence his exhortation to the Lord to pity Himself came. 'Get thee behind Me, Satan', showed that the Lord had traced this counsel to its true source. Whenever the supposed interests of self, or family, or country, or even of church or mission, come first, we may be quite sure of the true source of such counsel.

2. Blessed Prosperity

Blessed is the man that walketh not in the counsel of the
ungodly, nor standeth in the way of sinners,
nor sitteth in the seat of the scornful (Psalm 1:1).

The way of the sinner no more suits a true believer than the way
of the believer suits the sinner. As a witness for his Master in the
hope of saving the lost, he may go to them, but he will not, like
Lot, set his tent towards Sodom. Ah, how many parents who
have fluttered moth-like near the flame have seen their children
destroyed by it, while they themselves have not escaped unscathed.
And how many churches and Christian institutions, in the attempt
to attract the unconverted by worldly inducements and amusements,
have themselves forfeited the blessing of God, and have so lost
spiritual power that those whom they have attracted have been
nothing benefited. Instead of seeing the dead quickened, a state
of torpor and death has crept over themselves. There is no need of,
nor room for, any other attraction than that which Christ Himself
gave when He said: 'I, if I be lifted up, will draw all men unto
Me.' Our Master was ever 'separate from sinners', and the Holy
Spirit unmistakably says: 'What fellowship hath righteousness with
unrighteousness, and what communion hath light with darkness?'

'Nor sitteth in the seat of the scornful.' The seat of the scornful
is one of the special dangers of this age. Pride, presumption, and
scorn are closely linked together, and are far indeed from the
mind which was in Christ Jesus. This spirit often shows itself in
the present day in the form of irreverent criticism; those who are
least qualified for it are found sitting in the seat of judgment,
rather than taking the place of the inquirer and the learner. The
Bereans of old did not scornfully reject the, to them, strange
teachings of the Apostle Paul, but searched the Scriptures daily
to see whether these things were so. Now, forsooth, the Scriptures
themselves are called in question, and the very foundations of
Christian faith are abandoned by men who would fain be looked
upon as the apostles of modern thought.

3. Blessed Prosperity

His delight is in the law of the LORD; and in His law
doth he meditate day and night (Psalm 1:2).

We have noted the things avoided by the truly blessed man. We
now have to dwell upon the special characteristic of the man of
God, one which is at once his source of strength and his shield
of protection. The unregenerate cannot delight in the law of the
Lord. They may admire the Bible and be loud in its praises – for
it is the most wonderful book in the world. But when they become
converted they discover that they have got a new Bible.

It is not difficult to discover what a man delights in. 'Out of
the abundance of the heart the mouth speaketh.' The mother
delights to speak of her babe, the politician loves to talk of politics,
the scientific man of his favourite science, and the athlete of his
sport. In the same way the earnest, happy Christian manifests
his delight in the Word of God. Naturally and spontaneously he
will often speak of it.

The words, 'the law of the Lord', which we understand to
mean the whole Word of God, are very suggestive. They indicate
that the Bible is intended to teach us what God would have us to
do: that we should not merely seek for the promises, and try to
get all we can from God. It is recorded of Ezra, that he prepared
his heart to seek the law of the Lord in order that he might do it,
and teach in Israel statutes and judgments. The result was that
the hand of God was upon him for good.

But not only will the Bible become the law of the Lord to him as
teaching and illustrating what God would have *him* to be and to
do, but still more as revealing what God Himself is and does.
The man of God will also delight to trace God in the Word as the
great Worker, and rejoice in the privilege of being a fellow-worker
with Him. He himself and a thousand of his fellow-workers may
pass away; but this thought will not paralyse his efforts; for he
knows that what has been wrought in God will abide, and whatever
is incomplete the Great Worker will bring to completion.

4. Blessed Prosperity

He shall be like a tree planted by the rivers of water, that bringeth forth his fruit in his season; his leaf also shall not wither; and whatsoever he doeth shall prosper (Psalm 1:3).

This is one of the most remarkable and inclusive promises contained in the Scriptures. If we could offer to the ungodly a worldly plan which would ensure their prospering in all that they undertake, how eagerly would they undertake it! And yet when God reveals so effectual a plan to His people how few avail themselves of it! Many fail on the negative side and do not come clearly out of the world; many fail on the positive side and allow other duties and indulgences to take the time that should be given to the Word of God. To some it is not at all easy to secure time for the morning watch, but nothing can make up for the loss of it.

Let us now consider what are the blessings. 1. *Stability.* He shall be like a tree (not a mere annual) of steady, progressive growth and increasing fruitfulness. 2. *Independent supplies.* Planted by the rivers of water. The ordinary supplies of rain and dew may fail, his deep and hidden sources cannot. 3. *Seasonable fruitfulness.* There is something very beautiful in this. The figure is not that of water flowing through a channel; but of fruit, the very outcome of our own transformed life – a life of union with Christ. It is so gracious of God not to work through us in a mere mechanical way, but to make us branches of the true Vine, the very organ by which its fruit is produced.

There is a fundamental difference between fruit and work. Work is the outcome of effort; fruit of life. A bad man may do good work, but a bad tree cannot bear good fruit. The result of work is not reproductive, but fruit has its seed in itself. It is interesting to notice that the Scriptures do not speak of the fruits of the Spirit in the plural, as though we might take our choice among the graces named, but of the fruit in the singular, which is a rich cluster, composed of love, joy, peace, long-suffering, etc. How blessed to bring forth such fruit in its season!

5. Blessed Prosperity

His leaf also shall not wither; and whatsoever
he doeth shall prosper (Psalm 1:3).

Let us continue to consider what are the blessings, the manifold
happinesses, which faith is to claim when the conditions are
fulfilled.

Continuous vigour. 'His leaf shall not wither.' In our own
climate many trees are able to retain their leaves. The hardy
evergreen, however, not only lives, but maintains its leaf, and all
the more conspicuously because of the naked branches around.
The life within is too strong to fear the shortened day, the cold
blast, or the falling snow. So with the man of God whose life is
maintained by communion; adversity only brings out the strength
and reality of the life within. The leaf of the tree is no mere
adornment. If the root suggests receptive power, the leaves no
less remind us of the grace of giving and of purifying. The thin,
stimulating sap that comes from the root could not of itself build
up the tree. Through the leaves it possesses itself of carbon from
the atmosphere. The tiniest rootlets are as much nourished by the
leaves as the latter are fed by the roots. Keep a tree despoiled of
its leaves and it will surely die. 'His leaf shall not wither.'

Uniform prosperity. 'Whatsoever he doeth shall prosper.'
Could any promise go beyond this? It is the privilege of the
child of God to see the hand of God in all his circumstances,
and to serve God in all his avocations and duties. And he who
in all things recognises himself as the servant of God may count
on a sufficiency from God for all manner of need.

But this prosperity will not always be apparent, except to
the eye of faith. Doubtless the legions of hell rejoiced when
they saw the Lord of Glory nailed to the accursed tree, yet we
know that never was our blessed Lord more prospered than when
He offered Himself as our atoning sacrifice. The path of real
prosperity will often lie through deepest suffering; but followers
of Christ may well be content with the path He trod.

1. Blessed Adversity

The LORD gave, and the LORD hath taken away;
blessed be the Name of the LORD (Job 1:21).

All God's dealings are full of blessing: He is good, and doeth good, good only, and continually. The believer who has taken the Lord as his Shepherd, can assuredly say in the words of the Psalmist: 'Surely goodness and mercy shall follow me all the days of my life'. Hence we may be sure that days of adversity, as well as days of prosperity, are full of blessing. The believer does not need to wait until he sees the reason of God's afflictive dealings with him ere he is satisfied; he *knows* that all things work together for good to them that love God.

The history of Job is full of instruction, and should teach us many lessons of deep interest and profit. The veil is taken away from the unseen world, and we learn much of the power of our great adversary, but also of his powerlessness apart from the permission of God our Father.

Satan would very frequently harass the believer in times of sorrow and trial by leading him to think that God is angry with him. But our Heavenly Father delights to trust a trustworthy child with trial. Take the case of Abraham: God so trusted him that He was not afraid to call upon His servant to offer up his well-beloved son. And in the case of Job, it was not Satan that challenged God about Job, but God who challenged the arch-enemy to find any flaw in his character. In each case grace triumphed, and in each case patience and fidelity were rewarded.

The reply of Satan is noteworthy. He *had* considered God's servant, and evidently knew all about him. The arch-enemy had found all his own efforts ineffectual to harass and lead astray God's beloved servant. He had found a hedge around him, and about his servants, and about his house, and about all that he had on every side. How blessed to dwell so protected.

Is there no analogous spiritual blessing to be enjoyed nowadays? Thank God there is. Every believer may be as safely kept and as fully blessed.

2. Blessed Adversity

The LORD gave, and the LORD hath taken away;
blessed be the Name of the LORD (Job 1:21).

The great accuser having no fault to find with Job's character or
life, insinuates that it is all the result of selfishness. 'Doth Job
fear God for nought?' Indeed he did not, as Satan well knew!
Nor has anyone, before or since. There is no service which pays
so well as the service of our Heavenly Master: there is none so
royally rewarded. Satan was making a true assertion, but the
insinuation – that it was for the *sake* of the reward that Job
served God, was not true. And to indicate the character of Job
himself, Satan is permitted to test Job.

And soon Satan shows the malignity of his character by
bringing disaster after disaster upon the devoted man. But God
who sent the trial gave also the needful grace, and Job replied:
'The Lord gave, and the Lord hath taken away; blessed be the
Name of the Lord.'

Was not Job mistaken? Should he not have said: 'The Lord
gave, and Satan hath taken away?' No, there was no mistake.
He was enabled to discern the hand of God in all these calamities.
Satan himself did not presume to ask God to be allowed *himself*
to afflict Job. He says to God: 'Put forth *Thine* hand now, and
touch all that he hath, and he will curse Thee to Thy face'. And
again: 'Put forth Thine hand now, and touch his flesh and bone,
and he will curse Thee to Thy face'. Satan knew that none but
God could touch Job, and Job was quite right in recognising the
Lord Himself as the doer. Oftentimes shall we be helped and
blessed if we bear this in mind – that Satan is *servant*, and not
master, and that he, and wicked men incited by him, are only
permitted to do that which God by His determined counsel and
foreknowledge had before determined should be done. Come
joy or come sorrow, we may always take it from the hand of
God.

3. Blessed Adversity

The LORD gave, and the LORD hath taken away;
blessed be the Name of the LORD (Job 1:21).

Job's kinsfolk failed him, and his familiar friends seem to have forgotten him. Those who dwelt in his house counted him as a stranger, and his servants gave no answer to his calls. Worse than all, his own wife turned from him. No wonder that those who looked on thought that God Himself had become his enemy.

Yet it was not so. With a tender Father's love God was watching all the time; and when the testing had lasted long enough the temporary trial gave place to songs of deliverance.

Nor was the blessing God gave to His servant a small one. During this time of affliction Job learned lessons which all his life of prosperity had been unable to teach him. The mistakes he made in the hastiness of his spirit were corrected; the knowledge of God was deepened and increased. He exclaimed that he had heard of Him previously, and knew God by hearsay only, but that now his eye saw Him, and his acquaintance with God had become personal knowledge. And after all this, Job lived one hundred and forty years, and saw his children and his grandchildren to the fourth generation.

May we not well say that if Job's prosperity was blessed prosperity, his adversity, likewise, was blessed adversity? 'Weeping may endure for a night, but joy cometh in the morning'; and the night of weeping will bear a fruit more rich and permanent than any day of rejoicing. Light out of darkness is God's order.

In this day, when material causes are so much dwelt upon that there is a danger of forgetting the unseen agencies, let us not lose sight of our unseen foes. It would be comparatively easy to deal with our visible enemies, if the invisible foes were not behind them. We need to put on the whole armour of God, and not to be ignorant of Satan's devices. But let us not lose sight of the precious truth that God alone is Almighty. 'If God be for us, who can be against us?'

27th Day

Under the Shepherd's Care

For ye were as sheep going astray; but are now returned unto the Shepherd and Bishop of your souls (1 Peter 2:25).

This is evidently addressed to believers. We were like sheep, blindly, wilfully following an unwise leader. We turned every one to his own way. But we are now returned unto the Shepherd and Bishop of our souls. And it is so blessed to realize that now we are not without a Master, a Leader, a Head. We were intended to be followers. We always do follow; but, alas! we did not follow the right Master. And it is most restful now to realize that we are not left to live at the mercy of circumstances, or to walk in our own wisdom. We can never take in the future; we never fully take in the present.

How blessed to have such a Shepherd, Bishop, Overseer! I have frequently thought of the words uttered by Professor Charteris at a young men's Communion service in Edinburgh. He said that in the Lord Jesus we have a life of steady, uninterrupted development from the cradle to the Cross; but that it was the only life developed in that direction. The true Christian life always begins where His life ended, at the Cross; and the true development of the Christian life is to the cradle, until we can rest like babes in the omnipotent arms of infinite Wisdom and Love. The more we rest on this fact – that we do not know the way we are going, but that we have a Guide who does know, the more restful will our life become. We know not what burdens, perplexities, or difficulties the future may bring; but we know Him, whose we are, and whom we serve. He knows all; this suffices for us.

Are we all enjoying this precious truth? Are we able to say: I was a sheep going astray, but I am returned? If there be one who cannot do so, the Shepherd, the Bishop, is present, though unseen, to receive those who will return. If there is one burdened with sin, He is present to pardon. If there is one burdened with care, He is present to receive your care. He will be faithful to keep that which we commit to Him. May we be a docile flock, willing to be cared for.

And this is the law of the Nazarite, when the days of his separation are fulfilled: he shall be brought unto the door of the tabernacle of the congregation; And he shall offer his offering unto the Lord (Numbers 6:13-15).

We now come to the case of a Nazarite who has duly fulfilled his vow. He has now carried out all God's requirements, and his conscience is void of offence. Before God and man he is blameless. May he not now congratulate himself, and claim some measure of merit, seeing he has rendered to God an acceptable service, and among men has borne a consistent testimony? The offerings to be made on the conclusion of his vow – a burnt-offering, sin-offering, and a peace-offering – give an impressive answer to this question. They bring out the important difference between being *blameless* and being *sinless*. Having fulfilled the ordinance he was blameless; but the necessity alike for sin-offering, for burnt-offering, and for peace-offering, remind us of the sin of our holy things, and that not our worst, but our best, is only acceptable to God through the atonement of our Lord Jesus Christ.

While, however, the best services of the believer can neither give full satisfaction to his own enlightened conscience, nor be acceptable to God save through Jesus Christ, it is very blessed to know how fully all his needs are met in Christ, and how really he is accepted in Him, and enabled to give very real joy to God our Father which issues in the bestowal of His richest blessings. Very imperfect – sometimes worse than useless, is the effort of a little child to please and serve its parents; but where the parent sees real effort to do his will and to give him pleasure, is not the service gladly accepted, and the parent's heart greatly rejoiced? Thus it is our privilege to be Nazarites, only and always Nazarites, and through Christ Jesus to give joy and satisfaction by our imperfect service to our Heavenly Father.

The Secret of Fruitfulness

He that abideth in Me, and I in him, the same bringeth forth
much fruit; for without Me ye can no nothing (John 15:5).

Familiar as are these words, and dear to every Christian heart,
there are yet many by whom the topic of abiding in Christ (the
secret of fruitfulness) is not practically understood. We ourselves
look back on many sorrowful days of much discouragement,
for during the first twenty years of our Christian life we were
reading our thoughts into this chapter instead of gathering from
it Christ's meaning.

The first two words of the chapter: '*I am*', give us the key to
the whole secret of fruitfulness. 'I am the true Vine.' Not what
we are, but what *He* is; not what we do, but what His life works
in and through us. 'From Me is thy fruit found.' He is the true
Worker; He is the true Fruit-bearer.

'The *true* Vine.' The word rendered 'true', does not mean
true as opposed to false, but real as opposed to the type. The
vine was not borrowed to illustrate the truth, but it was created
to reveal the relationship of the Lord to His fruitbearing branches –
a relationship pre-existing in His own mind and purpose. This
important truth invests the vine with peculiar interest; and it opens
our eyes to see in many other earthly things, not merely God's
good gifts, but blessed revelations of the Creator Himself.

The true Vine. Let us note that Christ does not say that He is
the *Root* of the Vine, but the Vine itself – the whole tree. Some of
us have made the mistake of saying: How shall *I* get the fatness
out of the Root into my poor, puny branch? What is the Vine? Is
it not the *whole*, of which the roots and stem, branches and leaves,
are but parts? We have not to get anything *from* or *out of* Christ,
but *in* Christ to enjoy all His fulness. He has not *given* us life as
a gift; He Himself has *become* our life. 'When Christ who is our
life shall appear, then shall ye also appear with Him in glory.'
Not *from* Him, but *in* Him. Let us ever seek to realize Christ as
the whole Vine, apart from whom fruit-bearing is impossible.

The Reigning One

The Lord God Omnipotent reigneth (Revelation 19:6).

A glad day is coming! The voice of a great multitude, as the voice of many waters, and as the voice of mighty thunderings, will be heard saying: 'Alleluia! for the Lord God Omnipotent reigneth: let us be glad and rejoice and give honour to Him; for the marriage of the Lamb is come, and His wife hath made herself ready.' Then will be the great harvest home; and the innumerable throng, gathered out of all nations and kindreds and people and tongues, all clothed with white robes, and waving palms of victory, shall cry with loud voice: 'Salvation to our God which sitteth upon the throne, and unto the Lamb.'

'Blessed are they which are called unto the marriage supper of the Lamb!' Truly so: and will not those rejoice who have been the happy instruments used in calling them? If there could be sorrow in heaven, would it not be at the thought that some of the uncalled ones might have been called had we been more faithful to our Lord's commission, and had we at greater cost forwarded His work on earth?

Why do not more Christians gladly leave all and follow Christ in rescuing the perishing at any possible cost? Is it not because many of us, while looking forward to the future coming of His Kingdom, forget His present right to reign in the hearts of His own; and are unmindful of the blessed fact that *all* power is now given to Him, in heaven and in earth? Hence many never attempt to obey Him with unreserved consecration and trust, and live and act as if they were their own, and were at liberty to please themselves, and to give to God as much or as little service as they think fit, as much or as little of their time, strength, and possessions as is most agreeable to themselves. And *g-o*, to many, spells stay; or *y-e*, spells *somebody, anybody or nobody* as the case may be! Meanwhile the uncalled millions are dying without God; His command that the Gospel shall be preached to every individual is treated with contempt; and blood-guiltiness lies somewhere. Am I quite clear that none of it rests on me?

PART 3

THE LEGACY
OF HIS WORK

The Legacy of His Work

Remember them that were your leaders... imitate their faith
(Hebrews 13:7).

'I will open a way to the interior or perish.' So wrote Livingstone
of Africa. 'I feel as if I could not live if something is not done for
China.' So wrote Hudson Taylor concerning the land of Sinim.
Each man was 'a chosen vessel' to bear Christ's Name to the
nations. Each man received his own peculiar burden, and each
one died in the land of his adoption, the one in central Africa and
the other in the heart of China. But their eyes had 'seen the glory
of the coming of the Lord'.

'I have set thee down on purpose,' said a Voice to Bunyan,
'for I have something more than ordinary for thee to do'. It was
the same Voice that Paul heard, and it was the same Speakers
who spoke to Livingstone and to Hudson Taylor. 'Never shall I
forget the feeling that came over me,' wrote Hudson Taylor of
that experience. 'Words fail to describe it. I felt that I was in the
very presence of God, entering into covenant with the Almighty.'
That commission has never been withdrawn; the call to preach
the Gospel to every creature abides. The work then inaugurated
still awaits completion. 'He hath sounded forth the trumpet that
shall never call retreat.'

'I beg to direct your attention to Africa,' said Livingstone in
the closing sentences of his memorable speech at Cambridge on
December 3, 1857. 'I know,' he continued, 'that in a few years I
shall be cut off in that country, which is now open; do not let it be
shut again. I go back to Africa to make an open road for commerce
and Christianity; do you carry out the work which I have begun.
I leave it with you.' With these great words, bequeathing his
legacy to Christian England, Livingstone sat down. One who was
present has told us that the effect was tremendous. 'The speaker
had suddenly raised his voice to a shout – *I leave it with you* –
and then instantly stopped. It was as though a bomb had been

thrown into the Assembly.' That was Livingstone's legacy – Africa.

Hudson Taylor's legacy, though less dramatic in its presentation, was not less decisive. Livingstone founded no Society; in fact he retired from the one to which he at first belonged. He was a lonely man, ill-suited to co-operate with others. He was a giant path-finder, a pioneer, but no leader. Hudson Taylor, on the other hand, was essentially a great leader and hundreds volunteered to follow him as pioneers. And to those followers, now nearly twelve hundred in connection with the China Inland Mission alone, and to the innumerable friends and supporters in the many home lands, as well as to the Church at large, he has left this great unfinished task of the evangelization of China. 'The gifts and the calling of God are without repentance.'

The China Inland Mission as an organization has its carefully considered Constitution, its Principles and Practice, its Instructions to Probationers and Members, and its Declaration of Trust, all drawn up by Mr. Hudson Taylor himself to safeguard the Mission as an instrument for the evangelization of China. Such a Fellowship, so well fashioned to its end, was no small legacy in itself. He had no need, like Livingstone, to say at some farewell meeting: *I leave it with you.* He bequeathed the Work and an Organization into which he had breathed something of his own spirit.

But no one knew better than Hudson Taylor that spiritual inspiration was more than machinery. Though he had given meticulous care to the administration of the work, he knew that it was the Spirit alone who could quicken it. The body without life would be only a corpse, and an organization without the Breath of God would be worse than useless. It was this that led him, in the last official communication he ever wrote as General Director, to say, concerning the need of continual dependence upon God in all things, that 'should another spirit ever prevail, no rules could save the Mission, nor would it be worth saving. The China Inland Mission must be a living body in fellowship with God, or it will be no further use, and cannot continue.'

Mr. Taylor had a way of taking the public into his confidence, and of opening his heart to his hearers. Upon one such occasion he spoke more freely about the China Inland Mission than was even his wont, and we cannot do better than reproduce here part of what he then said.

'The thing that makes this work dear to our hearts is its connection with God and with Christ. It is for the glory of Christ: it is for the carrying out of His last command: it is for the glory of God. And it is just as a work of God that our confidence for the future, as our thankfulness for the past, is most called out.

'This work should not only be a work for China, but a work which may do each one of us good. Many people seem to be in a considerable measure of haze and doubt about spiritual realities, and therefore everything that comes to us, as it were, with a fresh voice from God – as a fresh evidence of the reality of His deep, unseen, blessed government, which we all rejoice in, and hold so firmly to – should be felt by us to be something of personal as well as of relative interest.

'It is my own most sincere desire that in this work God in all things should be glorified, that there should be no part of the work by which God cannot be glorified, that no part of it should continue any longer than God can be glorified thereby. It is either of Him, and for Him, and to His glory, or else it had better come to nought; and one of the things about the simple arrangements and organization that we have in this work which gives me more satisfaction than any other is this – it could not hold together for three months if the great mainstay – God's own faithfulness, God's own help, God's own power – were taken away. We have nothing else to depend upon, just as we have no one else to serve.

'Perhaps it is for His glory that I should refer a little, after so many years' experience of the work, to His personal dealings with me. [Here Mr. Taylor tells of his call, of his sailing in 1853 in connection with the Chinese Evangelization Society, and of his leaving that Society in 1857 because it was continually in debt.] From the day I took that step God blessed and helped me, and to this day I can testify to God's faithfulness. Faith has often been tried, but God has ever made these trials of faith such a real blessing to me that they have been among the chief means of grace to my own soul, as well as the chief help to my work.

'Having, then, this experience, we do not feel that we are wronging any brother or sister in saying: "My dear brother or sister, if you are satisfied God is calling you to go out and do a work for Him, do not expect that He will be less true to you than man would if he were to engage you to work for him." What should we think of the merchant who, though his clerk worked well, did not pay him his wages? Ought we to expect less of our God and our Father? Ought we not to believe that if we only are God-sent men and God-sent women, going to serve Him and not to please ourselves, going to follow His guidance and to do His work, He is *sure* to sustain us?

'If this is a real work for God it is a real conflict with Satan. I would not that we should underrate the powers of darkness. I am sure the great apostle of the Gentiles did not do so. Our warfare, he felt, was not with flesh and blood, but with wicked spirits – with spiritual wickedness – and it is with that spiritual wickedness that our conflict now is.

'I am not greatly concerned as to what may be the degree of demoralization of the people among whom we have to take the Gospel. If you could find a man or a woman anywhere so sunk that the regenerative power of the Holy Ghost was not able to make that man or woman new; if there were a man so degraded and so polluted that the cleansing power of the blood of Christ could not cleanse that person, then I think that we should have to form a very different estimate of the Gospel from that which, thank God, we are justified by His word in holding. I believe most thoroughly in the *power* of the blood of Christ – in the regenerative *power* of the Holy Ghost – in the *power* of the Gospel – that it is the *power of God* unto salvation to every one that believeth, no matter how sunken or degraded he may be.

'But, oh, my beloved friends, have we, the messengers – have we the grace to go to those sunken and degraded ones? Have we such a faith in God that *our* faith in Him shall not fail, that we shall not lack faith in that glorious *Gospel* that we have to preach to them? Have we the grace to cleave close to God in all and through all? *This is the thing that causes me concern, dear friends, and this is the thing about which I wish to ask your earnest prayers and your constant prayers.*'

'Life,' says a trenchant writer, 'seems to call for organization – and then dies of it'. Was this thought in Hudson Taylor's mind when he wrote the last words he ever penned as General Director? Those last words are these:

> 'I trust that in all the days to come, as in the past, we shall recognize our entire dependence upon God and the absolute importance of private and united prayer. How much blessing we owe to our days of prayer, our weekly and daily prayer-meetings, and those of the Councils, will never be known on earth.
>
> 'May God ever shine upon the Mission, and all connected with it at home and abroad, for Christ's sake.
>
> 'Yours ever gratefully and affectionately in Christ,
> J. Hudson Taylor.'

These words are from his last official Will and Testament. We have received the legacy of a great task, the legacy of a vast organization, and the legacy of a unique spirit. Yes, says the inspired writer, Remember and Consider, but 'Imitate the Faith'. This is the only way to conserve the past and to fulfil our inheritance. 'The information given in history is valueless in itself,' writes one of our great historians, 'unless it produces a new state of mind.' It is the mind that matters, the spirit that quickeneth. An accurate record of past events is, after all, only the shell of history. 'Collect the facts of the French Revolution!' says the same historian. How will you do it? 'You must go down to hell and up to heaven to fetch them.' In other words, mere externals do not give us the essence, the essentials. We should not be made musicians by possessing Mozart's or Beethoven's instruments. There is no real inheritance apart from the soul. 'Imitate their faith,' says the sacred writer. 'Be ye imitators of me,' says Paul, 'even as I also am of Christ.' Or, to revert again to the writer of the Epistle to the Hebrews: 'Be not sluggish, but imitators of them who through faith and patience inherit the promise.'

'No ideas will serve us long', wrote Bishop Westcott, 'till we have made them our own by serious effort.' This is one reason why we have sought to reproduce some of Mr. Hudson Taylor's messages in a way which will encourage a course of continued meditation. The best things cannot be automatically transferred. There is nothing so fatal as just to take things for granted. If we would enter into Hudson Taylor's legacy we must ponder long on the spiritual need and claims of China, we must meditate deeply on the promises of God, we must imitate his faith and venture all for God.

Not long ago, one who today bears heavy responsibilities in connection with the Mission, when commenting on the short life of Hudson Taylor, the volume entitled *Hudson Taylor: The Man who Believed God*, suddenly exclaimed, almost reproachfully, that it was not enough to write or to read about a man who believed God. What was essential was that we should all be men who believe God. This must be a common experience, not an exceptional one. Such a reminder is needed, for it is fatally easy to take this for granted.

Between the writing and the revising of these lines we have been meditating on the words of the Apostle Paul: 'We waxed bold in our God'. They have seemed so appropriate to our theme that we venture to close with them, for it was just this that characterized Hudson Taylor also. He waxed bold in his God, and if we would imitate his faith it is essential to remember this.

'But know', says the poet Herbert, in his *Church Porch*, 'that nothing can so foolish be as empty boldness: therefore first essay to stuff thy mind with solid bravery.' The word is apt if quaint in expression. Hudson Taylor's daring was not presumption; it had the solid ground of the knowledge of God. He waxed bold in God. 'We can never too often remember, nor too simply,' wrote the late Bishop Moule, 'that the true power of true Faith lies in its object. Therefore let us recollect the Object.' Here lies the secret of Hudson Taylor's faith and of his holy boldness. He knew God and was bold. 'Imitate their faith.'

'The people that know their God shall be strong and do exploits', was God's word to Daniel. This is the royal road the saints have trod. There is none other. Let us 'imitate their faith'.

'Come' and 'Go'

> Come unto Me, all ye that labour and are heavy laden,
> and I will give you rest (Matthew 11:28).

To every toiling, heavy-laden sinner, Christ says: 'Come unto Me ... and ... rest.'

But there are many toiling, heavy-laden believers too. For them also is this invitation meant. Note well the word of Jesus, if you are heavy-laden with your service, and do not mistake it. It is not: 'Go, labour on,' as perhaps you imagine. On the contrary it is stop, turn back, 'Come unto Me and rest.' Never, never did Christ send a heavy-laden one to work; never, never did He send a hungry one, a weary one, a sick or sorrowing one, *away* on any service. For such the Bible only says, 'Come, Come, Come.'

The first evangelist of the New Testament records the invitation on which we are writing. The last gives us the similar one: 'If any man thirst, let him come unto Me and drink.' The New Testament almost closes with the words: 'Let him that is athirst Come, and drink of the water of life freely.'

How many of the Lord's redeemed people have spent hours, or days, or even months, in sorrow and self-reproach from some imagined duty which they had not courage or strength to perform, heavy-laden all the time! How many can tell of the journey by omnibus or rail that was a time of intense distress, because they felt they ought to be speaking to their fellow-passengers about their souls, but could not. And how many have done *far worse*: have spoken, when they had no message from God, and have done harm rather than good. Oh! how different it would have been had they but first come to Jesus; found rest and living water; and then, when the waters were welling up within , the rivers would have flowed naturally and irrepressibly, and the happy countenance would have said more than the heartfelt words were uttering! No one would then have looked at the face of the speaker and *felt*, 'What a dreadful religion his must be!' For the 'Come' is not intended to exclude the 'Go', but to prepare the way for it.

2nd Day

Every Valley Shall Be Exalted

Every valley shall be exalted, and every
mountain and hill shall be made low (Isaiah 40:4).

These words, applicable to John the Baptist, whose work was preparatory to the first coming of Christ, are not less applicable to ourselves. No easy task was it in those days to 'prepare the way of the Lord'. And grave difficulties and great obstacles are frequently met with today. It is most important that we should view these from the right standpoint. How different an impression was produced on Caleb and Joshua by what they saw in the land of promise from that made on the minds of the other ten spies. While the ten compared the difficulties with the weakness of Israel, the two compared them with the might of Israel's God, and boldly asserted, 'We are well able to overcome... they are bread for us'. Every difficulty overcome by faith is bread.

If, then, God in His providence orders that our work shall lead to valleys of difficulty which we cannot bridge over, to mountainous obstacles which we have no means of surmounting, to crooked paths which the united zeal and energy of the Church cannot make straight, to rough places that no human power can make plain, shall we be discouraged? Shall we not bless and praise His holy name for a clear platform on which His holy arm, ever working, though hiddenly, can be made bare – on which all flesh, and not merely the enlightened believer, must see the manifestation of the glory of the Lord?

Are there not many of us who are distressingly conscious of deep valleys of deficiencies that we know not how to fill up? Lack of power, or courage, or faith? Are there not mountains and hills we cannot lay low? Fiery tempers, impetuous dispositions we have tried to curb in vain? The heart is lifted up with triumph, the lips are filled with praise, as we review in this light the mighty difficulties to be overcome – a whole host of difficulties, which would otherwise overwhelm the Christian missionary, now only serve to deepen his joy and to increase his assurance of ultimate triumph.

In nothing be anxious; but in everything by prayer and supplication with thanksgiving let your requests be made known unto God (Philippians 4:6).

I do want you, dear friend, to realize this principle of working with God and of asking Him for everything. If the work is at the command of God, then we can go to Him with full confidence for workers. And when God gives the workers, *then* we can go to Him for the means. We always accept a suitable worker, whether we have the funds or not. Then we very often say, 'Now, dear friend, your first work will be to join with us in praying for the money to send you to China.' As soon as there is money enough, the time of the year and other circumstances being suitable, the friend goes out. We do not wait until there is a remittance in hand to give him when he gets there. The Lord will provide that.

Our Father is a very experienced One: He knows very well that His children wake up with a good appetite every morning, and He always provides breakfast for them; and He does not send His children supperless to bed. 'Thy bread shall be given thee, and thy water shall be sure.' He sustained three millions of Israelites in the wilderness for forty years. We do not expect that He will send three million missionaries to China; but if He did, He would have plenty of means to sustain them all. Let us see that we keep God before our eyes; that we walk in His ways, and seek to please and glorify Him in everything. Depend upon it, God's work done in God's way will never lack God's supplies.

When the supplies do not come in, it is time to enquire, What is wrong? It may be only a temporary trial of faith; but if there be faith, it will bear trying, and if not it is well that we should not be deceived. It is very easy, with money in the pocket and food in the cupboard, to think you have faith in God. Miss Havergal says: 'Those who trust Him wholly find Him wholly true.' But my experience proves that to those who do not trust Him wholly, He does not break His word. 'He cannot deny Himself.'

God's Battle

> The battle is not yours, but God's. Tomorrow go ye down
> against them (2 Chronicles 20:15-16).

The history of Jehoshaphat is a very instructive one, for his life is often spiritually re-acted. A true-hearted man, he began his career well. But alas! a change came. Time would fail us to enumerate the calamities which followed the great mistake and sin of Jehoshaphat's life. But he and his people began to seek the Lord. Note the response: 'Thus saith the LORD: Be not afraid nor dismayed by reason of this great multitude, for the battle is not yours, but God's. Tomorrow go ye down against them .... Ye shall not need to fight in this battle: set yourselves, stand ye still, and see the salvation of the LORD... for the Lord is with you' (2 Chron. 20:16-17). What light can these words throw on the great problem of China's evangelization? We will seek with all brevity to indicate several lines of thought.

To whom were these words spoken? To a little band – in numbers small, in resources limited, in council feeble. Yet was the command given: 'Tomorrow go out against them.' They had appealed to God for help, and God had promised it. Nevertheless the command is given: 'Tomorrow go out'.

Note the prompt and immediate obedience required. They were not to wait for reinforcements on their own side, or for defections on the side of their foes. Therefore the word is: 'Tomorrow go out against them.'

See how Jehoshaphat obeyed, implicitly and without question. We hear nothing of reluctance to go out, of delays by the way.

Lastly, note how speedily was their faith honoured: how fully God delivered them, and how unprecedented were the means used.

Our command is to go into all the world and to preach to every creature. But we are a little band. Shall we wait for reinforcements, for further facilities, for enlarged resources? Or shall we not rather say: God is with us, and reckoning on His presence, go at once?

Whence should we have so much bread in the wilderness, so as
to fill so great a multitude? (Matthew 15:33).

It seems to me we need to ask more seriously than in by-gone
days, What is really the will and command of our blessed Lord?
and to set about obeying Him, not merely attempting to obey. I
do not know that we are told anywhere in the Bible to try to do
anything. 'We must try to do the best we can,' is a very common
expression; but I remember some years ago, after a remark of
that kind, looking very carefully through the New Testament to
see under what circumstances the disciples were told to *try* to do
anything. I was surprised that I did not find any instance. Then I
went through the Old Testament with the same result. There were
many commands apparently impossible to obey, but they were
all definite commands.

God gives His Spirit, not to those who long for Him, not to
those who pray for Him, not to those who desire to be filled
always; but He does give His Holy Spirit to them that *obey*
Him. A handful of meal blessed by the Lord is quite sufficient to
accomplish any purpose. He chooses to accomplish by it. It is
not a question of resources to all those who are following the
Master, who are doing just what He has for them to do.

There has come home to my heart, with a power I have never
realized before, the commission to 'preach the Gospel to every
creature', to the whole creation. It does seem to me we want to
take this command of rapid evangelization to our hearts, and
say, What did the Lord mean by saying, 'Preach the Gospel to
every creature'? The command really implies that each generation
shall evangelize its own generation; just as the multitude in our
Lord's day had an immediate supply for an immediate need. It
would have been useless to say to them: 'After two or three days
you shall be fed.' They were hungry, and would faint by the way.
So today, the multitude are perishing; and while we are waiting,
they are dying without the Gospel.

Tell It Out[1]

> Then I said, Here am I; send me. And He said,
> Go, and tell this people (Isaiah 6:8, 9).

Why, beloved friends, should we 'Tell it out among the heathen that the Lord is King'? Is it true? Do I believe it? Do you believe it? Am I ready to obey Him, even as King? Are you ready to obey Him as King? Beloved friends, let us be honest before God tonight. Is it true that the Lord is King? If it be, may God make us His faithful subjects, His obedient subjects.

'Tell it out among the heathen that the Saviour reigns.' Why should we tell it out among the heathen that the Saviour *reigns*? Does He reign? Is it true? If the Saviour reigns, why is it that we are all here tonight, and that there are men and women who have never heard of this Saviour? How about those who are perishing by millions through the famine in China? When the people are suffering in this way, 'Where is there a Saviour?' they ask. 'Does the Saviour live? Does He reign?' And are you here, beloved friends, tonight, with that cry ringing in your ears? Do not say to a few of us missionaries, 'Tell it out!' but ask yourselves, Is it true? Is it true that the Saviour reigns? Do not say it if you do not feel it; but if you do feel it, go and tell it out that He is a Saviour indeed, and let the world read in your life that there is a Saviour, and know that He reigns.

'Tell it out among the heathen, Jesus reigns above.' Oh beloved friends, if that Saviour is Jesus, the man Christ Jesus, the sympathizing Jesus, may God grant that some among us may hear His voice tonight. I ask these questions, because if neither you nor I doubt that the Lord is King, or that there is a Saviour and that He reigns, or that the Saviour's name is Jesus, then we individually have need of this Saviour, for we have not been obedient, and we have not told it out. Do not sing 'Waft, waft, ye winds, the story!' for the winds will not waft it; some of you must go and tell it.

---

1. These words were spoken after the singing of Miss Havergal's well-known hymn.

The Lord God Omnipotent Reigneth

And I heard as it were the voice of a great multitude, and as the
voice of many waters, and as the voice of mighty thunderings,
saying, Alleluia; for the Lord God omnipotent reigneth
(Revelation 19:6).

We must never forget three important statements. There is a God;
He has spoken to us in the Bible; He means what He says. The
missionary who realizes these truths knows that he has solid rock
under his feet whatever may be his circumstances and surroundings.
We all need, and always shall need, this confidence. It is no small
blessing when the glorious truth, 'The Lord God Omnipotent
reigneth', takes possession of the heart of the child of God.

But if it oftentimes needs no small faith to be triumphant when
the powers of evil are seen working around us, what shall we say
when we find them working within? No foe without can be as danger-
ous as a traitor inside the encampment. Who has not at some
time or other felt as if it would be easier to die for God a Christian's
death, than to live for God a Christian's life? Are we not often
tempted to lower the Christian standard and to call some sins by
pleasant-sounding names – weakness, failure, infirmities – or,
seeing them in their true colours, to give way almost to despair?

Is there no remedy? Must we either accept the unscriptural
idea that practically sin must reign, or the equally unscriptural
idea that before the redemption of the purchased possession we
may get rid of sin altogether, root and branch? No; we are not
shut up to these alternatives! There is a remedy; and that remedy
is the Lord Jesus Christ. Christ for us, as our Paschal Lamb;
Christ with us, to order all our goings, as the cloud led the Israelites;
Christ in us, able to take possession, and able to keep possession.

If this indeed be so, missionaries abroad, and their friends at
home, equally need to apprehend it. We are more than fellow-
workers: we are members of the one body. If the Mighty One be
indeed within us, we need not fear the greatness of the enterprise.
We may dare to obey His command.

And there shall be with thee for all manner of workmanship
every willing skilful man, for any manner of service: also the
princes and all the people will be wholly at thy commandment
(1 Chronicles 28:21).

We know of no promise more encouraging to the Christian worker
than that given to Solomon in connection with the building of the
Temple. The true Solomon is on the throne, and the building of
the true temple is in progress, and to Him is promised every
willing skilful man for service, and the princes of the house of
God and all the people to be at His commandment.

It sometimes seems as if there were willing workers who were
not skilful, and skilful workers who might be more willing. How
are we to secure for the work of God the beautiful combination –
willing skilful men? It is to our Royal Master they are promised.
From Him they must be sought; must be claimed by faith and
prayer, as Christ Himself directed His disciples to pray to the
Lord of the harvest to thrust forth labourers into His own harvest.

Adopting this course from the commencement, we can bear
our testimony to His faithfulness in supplying willing skilful men
for very varied departments of work. From the anvil and the
plough, from the counter and the desk, from the college and the
university, from the mansion and the hall, He has sent forth willing
skilful workers fitted for varying departments of service. Each
one has been a blessing, and each one has been blessed. As
Jonathan beautifully said to his armour-bearer: 'There is no
restraint to the Lord to save by many or by few.' He can use the
talents and culture of a Paul, if Paul has been crucified with
Christ, though He more commonly speaks by an unlettered Peter
as at Pentecost. He can use the wealth of a David, when there is
David's largeness of heart. But oftentimes His mightiest works
are wrought by those who can exclaim, 'Silver and gold have I
none; but such as I have give I thee. In the name of Jesus Christ
of Nazareth rise up and walk'.

The Joy of the LORD is your Strength (Nehemiah 8:10).

There are few things more attractive than joy – and few are more communicative. We are instinctively drawn to persons possessed of a happy countenance and a bright, cheery manner. Over the young especially, a joyful countenance and cheerful manner exert a powerful influence. True wisdom is 'rejoicing always before Him', and neutralizing the devil's lie, that the service of God is a gloomy thing.

It is one of the striking evidences of the love of God, that He has so secured the existence and wide diffusion of joy, that even in this sin-stricken world it is everywhere to be found. The young of all animals are naturally joyous; health and vigour make even toil a pleasure; and the lawful exercise of every faculty with which God has endowed us tends to the increase of our joy. The birds of the air, the flowers of the field, the wild rolling ocean, and the stable glorious hills, are all sources of joy; and every social and domestic relationship of life tends to increase the sum of human happiness. It is quite clear that the God of creation would have His creatures joyful.

Not only does nature teach us that it must be the will of our Father that His children especially should be a joyful family, but the Old and New Testaments are full of encouragements, and even commands, to lead rejoicing lives. In the revival recorded in Nehemiah we find that the people were overwhelmed by the contrast between their individual and national lives and the requirements of God. But those who taught the people said, 'This day is holy unto the LORD your God. Mourn not, nor weep;... go your way, eat the fat and drink the sweet, and send portions unto them for whom nothing is prepared;... neither be ye sorry, for the joy of the LORD is your strength.' And the people went their way and rejoiced accordingly. Joy is of God.

2. Strength for Service

The Joy of the LORD is your Strength (Nehemiah 8:10).

What is the joy of the Lord? Is it joy that there *is* such a Lord? for we cannot *realize* His existence without joy. Or, is it joy that He is *our* Lord? For possession is a fruitful source of joy. Or, again, is it joy that He has *imparted* to us, and shed abroad in our hearts by His Spirit? Or, lastly, is it His *own* joy which is our strength? We feel no doubt that, while all these sources of joy are ours, it is to the last of them that this passage specifically refers.

John 15:11 refers to our Saviour's *joy in fruit-bearing*, through His branches. It was His will that *His* joy might remain in them; and that consequently *their* joy might be full. Here we see the joy of the Lord distinguished from the joy of His people.

In Hebrews 12:2, we have the joy of the Lord in the redemption of His people – joy to despise the shame and endure the cross. It was strength for self-sacrifice.

In Zephaniah 3:17, we have the joy of the Lord in the possession of His purchased inheritance. Oh, how wonderful is this joy! 'He will rejoice over thee with joy, He will rest in His love, He will joy over thee with singing.'

It is the consciousness of the threefold joy of the Lord – His joy in ransoming us; His joy in dwelling within us as our Saviour and Power for fruitbearing; and His joy in possessing us, as His Bride and His delight – it is the consciousness of this joy which is our real strength. Our joy in Him may be a fluctuating thing: His joy in us knows no change.

Are we living in the daily, hourly enjoyment of this strength? Is the unconscious, but irrepressible manifestation of this enjoyment ever speaking well of our Master? Are tell-tale faces and tell-tale eyes bearing witness that the Lord is good, where no word is uttered? Is this life-testimony felt at home, in our own family circles? And can we appeal to those most intimate with us, as Paul did? – 'Ye know after what manner I have been with you at *all* seasons.'

11th Day

The Knowledge of God

This is life eternal, that they should know Thee, the only true God (John 17:3).

There is a far closer connection than we sometimes realize between the knowledge of God and practical use of that knowledge. It is just as we are faithfully living out the life He has put us in, and faithfully using the knowledge given to us, that we learn practically to know Him. We cannot separate these things. If we want to know the power of His resurrection, we must also know the fellowship of His sufferings, being made comfortable to His death. There must be the living out of the life of God in order that we may learn to know Him more fully and perfectly. We only know and understand that through which we have passed. It is in carrying this Gospel throughout the world, in manifesting it at home and abroad, that we shall realize and learn to know God. As we become like Him, we shall understand Him.

Thirty-one years ago I was leaving the shores of England for China. My beloved and honoured, and now sainted, Mother went down to Liverpool with me. I shall never forget that day when I sailed for China – how that loved Mother went with me into the little cabin that was to be my home for nearly six months. We parted, and she went on shore, giving me her blessing. I stood on the deck, and she followed the ship as we moved toward the dock gates. As we passed the gates, and the separation was commencing, I shall never forget the cry of anguish that was wrung from that Mother's heart as she felt that I was gone. It went to my heart like a knife. I never knew so fully as then what 'God so loved the world' meant; and I am quite sure that my precious Mother learned more of the love of God for the world in that hour than in all her life before.

Oh friends! when we are brought into the position of having practical fellowship with God in trial and sorrow and suffering, we learn a lesson that is not to be learnt amidst the ease and comfort of ordinary life. This is why God so often brings us through trying experiences.

117

ˈ

The LORD God is a Sun and Shield: the LORD will give grace and glory: no good thing will He withhold from them that walk uprightly (Psalm 84:11).

The Lord God is a Sun and Shield, and this in the fullest conceivable sense. None of His works can fully reveal the great Designer, the Executer and Upholder; and the loftiest thoughts and imaginations of the finite mind can never rise up to and comprehend the Infinite. The natural sun is inconceivably great, we cannot grasp its magnitude; it is inconceivably glorious, we cannot bear to gaze on one ray of its untempered light. And yet it may be the very smallest of all the countless suns that God has made! What of the glorious Maker of them all!

The Lord God is a Sun. He is the Reality of all that sun or suns suggest. My reader, is He the Sun to you?

And the Lord God is a Shield. Dangers encompass us at every moment. Within us and around us are dangers unseen which at any moment might terminate our earthly career. Why do we live so safely then? Because the Lord God *is* a Shield. The world, the flesh, and the devil are very real; and unaided we have no power to keep or deliver ourselves from them. But the Lord God *is* a Shield. It is a small thing then to go to China, a very small additional risk to run; for there as here the Lord God *is* a Shield. To know and do His will – this is our safety and rest.

Sweet are His promises – grace will He give and glory. Grace all unmerited and free. And glory too – glory *now*, the glory of being His, of serving Him, and glory in the soul. No good thing will He withhold from them that walk uprightly. Ah! how often when we have been dissatisfied with the ways of God, we ought to have been dissatisfied with our own ways.

But sweet as are God's promises, the Promiser is greater and better. Hence if we had claimed all the promises, and had opened our mouths wide, He would still be able to do exceedingly above all we ask or think. He delights to do so.

13th Day

The Certainty of Divine Things

From an article written after the sailing of The Hundred.

Now that the number is complete, we may well look back, grateful for the manifest answer to prayers, and ponder a few of the questions their going forth suggests.

They have gone in glad obedience. The Master said Go! and they have gladly gone. They did not need to ask Why? His word sufficed. To 'The Hundred' the words Go and Stay had not a letter in common.

They have gone in fullest confidence. They never asked, Is His command a wise one or a kind one? To them He is wisdom, He is love. When He gave the command He knew all involved to those who go, to those they leave, to those among whom they will labour.

They have gone without anxiety. There would be no step of the way unknown to Him. They went not alone: He was with them alway, and would be with them. All authority on earth, as surely as in heaven, is given unto Him.

They have gone to do a definite work. Not to try this, or that, but to do, in the strength of the Lord, what He has told them. They know that divine commands mean divine enablings.

Do we not need to dwell more frequently on the certainty, the absolute certainty of divine things? Why is gravitation certain? Because it is a divine law. Why is Scripture just as certain? Because it is a divine Word. Why is prayer offered in the Name of Christ as certain to be answered as the sun is to rise? Because both are according to the divine Will: both are promised in the Scriptures.

In that Book of certainties we see unmistakably the woeful position of the heathen, and can well see why the command to evangelize them all is given. If we could not see, it would, nevertheless, be our duty, or let us say our privilege, to obey. But our Master treats us as friends, and tells us His reasons – and one of them is the awful position of the heathen. Is it not for Him to decide whether we, or our loved ones, serve Him at home or abroad.

God's Everlasting Kingdom

His Kingdom is an everlasting Kingdom, and His
dominion is from generation to generation (Daniel 4:3).

We do not often quote the words of a heathen monarch as the text
of a sermon, but the noble confession of Nebuchadnezzar may
well suggest many helpful thoughts to us – thoughts, too, as
encouraging as they are helpful. It is a prolific cause of much
failure and loss, of much discouragement and inactivity, to
realize insufficiently the truth that the Lord is King. No small
part of the failure of Christianity to claim long ago – and today –
the people of all nations for our Master may be traced to this one
error. It is all-pervading in its injurious effects, and to remove
them we need to remove the cause.

How seldom do we hear the expression 'the Gospel *of the
Kingdom*' used, and when used how often it is evidently little
more than a meaningless phrase! And yet how full is the Word
of God of the blessings brought by and enjoyed under His rule.
Let us then prize this great truth of the Kingship of the Lord
Jesus, meditate upon it, act upon it.

The New Testament as well as the Old bears abundant witness
to it. The angel announced before His birth, 'The Lord God
shall give Him the throne of His Father David, and He shall
reign over the house of Jacob for ever, and of His Kingdom there
shall be no end.' To Pilate the Lord Himself bore witness: 'My
Kingdom is not of this world.' 'Art Thou a King then?' 'To this
end was I born.' Born to reign, He acted consistently through
His life of ministry. As a King He called His apostles
authoritatively to leave their properties and employments and
follow Him. As a King He laid down the laws of the Kingdom in
the Sermon on the Mount. And as a King He despatched His
ambassadors to preach the Gospel of the Kingdom. With royal
dignity He witnessed before His sacrificial death to His
Kingship; the title over the Cross proclaimed it, and He was
raised as Prince and Saviour. Blessed are those servants whom
the Lord, when He cometh, shall find watching.

Fasting and Prayer

This kind can come out by nothing, save by prayer and fasting
(Mark 9:29).

In Shansi I found Chinese Christians who were accustomed, not
infrequently, alone and together, to spend time in fasting and
prayer. They recognised that this fasting, which so many dislike,
which requires faith in God, since it makes one feel weak and
poorly, is really a divinely appointed means of grace. Perhaps
the greatest hindrance to our work is our own imagined strength;
and in fasting we learn what poor, weak creatures we are –
dependent on a meal of meat for the little strength which we are
so apt to lean upon. However the blessing comes, this I know;
we do find that when we have a serious difficulty in the China
Inland Mission, and set apart a day of fasting (we have had very
many) God always interposes. He goes before us, and makes crooked
places straight; He goes before us, and makes rough places plain.

If this principle of taking everything to, and accepting
everything from, God is a true one – I think the history of the
China Inland Mission proves that it is – ought we not to bring it
to bear more and more in daily life? The Lord's will is that all
His people should be an unburdened people, fully supplied, strong,
healthy and happy. Obey in faith the conditions of the 1st Psalm,
and you will surely be prosperous in all that you do – in everything
domestic, in every business transaction, as well as in every
spiritual service. It is the Lord's will that His people should be as
the children of a king. Shall we not determine to 'be careful for
nothing, but in everything by prayer and supplication with
thanksgiving' bring those things that would become burdens or
anxieties to God in prayer. 'If we believe not, He abideth faithful;
He cannot deny Himself.'

God's Universities

A vessel unto honour, sanctified, meet for the Master's use,
prepared unto every good work (2 Timothy 2:21).

Another principle on which we have worked in the China Inland
Mission, has not disappointed us. We have accepted the workers
God gave us, though they have been of very different qualif-
ications. The man who would attempt to build a hall without an
architect would not be very wise. But it would be quite as great
a mistake to say, because architects are needed, 'We will have
none but architects'. And so in missionary efforts men who have
gone through a valuable curriculum of study are very few, and
the number willing and able to go out is insufficient, if that were
all. But, apart from this, there is much work in the mission field
that others can do positively better. God has adapted each one to
his own work. A bricklayer will build better than an architect;
and an architect will superintend, and make plans, better than a
bricklayer. It is in the combination of 'willing skilful' workers,
suited to every department of service, that the work of God will
go on as it ought to do. What church would insist on having
ordained men to teach the alphabet in a Sunday-school?

God has given us men of the highest ability; but we have
others who have graduated in different schools. Is there not a
lesson to be learnt here? We must not reject God-given men
because they have been brought up in different social circles,
and have had different educational advantages. I say *different
advantages*, for I hold it to be sheer infidelity to doubt that God
gives to every one of His children, without exception, those
circumstances which are to him the highest educational
advantages that he can improve, and that will best suit him for
his own work. There is a school of sorrow, as Pastor Hsi
reminded us in Shansi. There is a school of trial and persecution;
and men who have not graduated in that school do not prove
very good helpers for the churches.

Ah, dear friends, God has His own universities, and His way
of training men.

God's Guarantees

Seek ye first His Kingdom and His righteousness; and all these things shall be added unto you (Matthew 6:33).

We concluded to invite the co-operation of fellow-believers, irrespective of denomination, who fully believed in the inspiration of God's Word, and were willing to prove their faith by going into Inland China with only the guarantees they carried within the covers of their pocket Bibles. God had said, 'Seek ye first the Kingdom of God and His righteousness, and all these things (food and raiment) shall be added unto you.' If anyone did not believe that God spoke the truth, it would be better for him not to go to China to propagate the faith. If he did believe it, surely the promise sufficed.

Again, 'No good thing will He withhold from them that walk uprightly.' If anyone did not mean to walk uprightly, he had better stay at home; if he did mean to walk uprightly, he had all he needed in the shape of a guarantee fund. God owns all the gold and silver in the world, and the cattle on a thousand hills. We need not be vegetarians.

Money wrongly placed, and money given from wrong motives, are both to be greatly dreaded. We can afford to have as little as the Lord chooses to give; but we cannot afford to have unconsecrated money, or to have money placed in the wrong position. Far better have no money at all, even to buy food with, for there are ravens in China which the Lord could send again with bread and flesh. The Lord is always faithful; He tries the faith of His people, or rather their faithfulness. People say, 'Lord, increase our faith.' Did not the Lord rebuke His disciples for that prayer? He said, 'You do not want a great faith, but faith in a great God. If your faith were as small as a grain of mustard-seed, it would suffice to remove this mountain!' We need a faith that rests on a great God, and which expects Him to keep His word, and to do just what He has promised.

Let Thy work appear unto Thy servants, and Thy glory unto their children. And let the beauty of the LORD our God be upon us; and establish Thou the work of our hands (Psalm 90:16-17).

The desire to be prosperous in our worldly callings and in our spiritual enterprises is a most natural one, and there are few who are not prepared to unite in the last petition of the Ninetieth Psalm. This petition is perfectly legitimate if kept in its proper place. It is to be noted, however, that it is not found in the first verse of the Psalm, but in the last. If it take the same place in our hearts that it had in the prayer of Moses, it will be a safe one for us to offer.

The history of Moses is very instructive. He was not a young man when he first essayed to deliver Israel; nor, as men would say, unequipped and untrained. Yet he lacked the necessary spiritual preparation. He had not come to the end of the self, and hence he failed. He went forward 'supposing'. Humbled and instructed by his failure, he did not again attempt their deliverance until it was pressed upon him by God Himself.

Mere deliverance from evil and from sorrow might lead to a self-satisfied life, devoid of knowledge of or interest in the great purposes of God. Hence he prays, 'Let Thy work appear ... and Thy glory.'

The prayer is not less appropriate in our own day than it was in the time of Moses. And Moses prays, 'And let the beauty of the Lord our God be upon us.' Let it not merely be revealed to us, but let it be reflected by us, let it rest upon us. And when Moses came down from the mount the beauty of the Lord was upon him, so his prayer is that all the people of God may reflect the beauty of His character.

Shall not we be more concerned that the beauty of the Lord our God be upon us than that our work be established? Let this be the primary object. Then come in their proper place the petitions: 'Establish Thou the work of our hands upon us; yea, the work of our hands establish Thou it.'

To Every Creature

Go ye into all the world, and preach the Gospel to every creature
(Mark 16:15).

How are we going to treat the Lord Jesus Christ in reference to this command? Shall we definitely drop the title Lord as applied to Him, and take the ground that we are quite willing to recognize Him as Saviour, so far as the eternal penalty of sin is concerned, but are not prepared to recognize ourselves as bought with a price, or Him as having any claim to our unquestioning obedience? Shall we say that we are our own masters, willing to recognize something as His due, provided He does not ask too much?

The heart of every true Christian will unhesitatingly reject this proposition when so formulated. But have not countless lives in each generation been lived as though it were a proper ground to take? How few of the Lord's people have recognized the truth that Christ is either Lord of all, or is not Lord at all. 'Why call ye Me, Lord, Lord, and do not the things that I say?' Shall it not become a holy ambition to all who have health and youth to court the Master's approval and tread in His steps, in seeking to save a lost world? And shall not Christian parents encourage their enthusiasm?

There is no impossibility in our Master's command. Were a great Government to determine on the conquest of a distant land they would think it a small matter to land ten thousand troops in any part of the world; and the Church of God today could easily, within the next five years, effect the evangelization of every one of China's millions.

It must not be forgotten that The Opener, who still holds the key of David, has given His word of promise to be with such workers 'all the days'. And no such effort could be made without an out-pouring of the Holy Spirit on the Church universal, which would include the Christian Churches of China, and make tens of thousands of Chinese Christians a mighty power for the evangelization of their own people. Let us not forget that to preach the Gospel to every creature is not a mere human project but a *divine command*.

I will go in the strength of the Lord (Psalm 71:16).

The world seems going on at an almost maddening rate, and the long-closed heathen empires have been marvellously opened to the missionary. But Satan still reigns; the god of this world is not dethroned. Increasing knowledge of science has increased the fearful power of our weapons of destruction, and the armed millions indicate but too plainly that man fears man no less, and loves man no more.

Who can foresee the events and changes which a few years may bring should our Lord delay His coming? We truly live in perilous times, whether we look at things political or things religious. Never was there a time in which it was more important to walk with God and to abide in the secret place of the Most High, nor in which it was more urgent to be up and doing. Shall we not, at this important epoch, remind ourselves afresh of our acceptance in and through Him, and of our privilege to present ourselves as living sacrifices to Him? In the measure in which we truly recognize Him as our Lord and ourselves as His possession will it be easy to 'put our trust' in Him. Do we not all take the charge of those things which we have purchased? If the shepherd purchase a flock of sheep, does he not intend to provide for and take care of them? And the more they cost the more carefully will he tend them. Well may we 'put our trust' in Him who loves us with love so unique and unparalleled! Then having afresh 'put our trust' in Him, let us further 'go in the strength of the Lord God'.

The rest of faith is not the rest of apathy or inaction. The more God enlarges the work, the more earnestly and constantly will the enemy attempt to hinder and mar. Pray that He will speedily open the whole of the country to aggressive missionary work, and that He will speedily thrust forth large bands of evangelists *determined* to reach every family. Exulting faith will go in the strength of the Lord singing: 'If God be for us, who can be against us?'

21st Day

Our Father which art in heaven, Hallowed be
Thy Name, Thy Kingdom come! (Matthew 6:9).

When our Lord taught us to say: 'Our Father which art in heaven,
hallowed be Thy Name, Thy Kingdom come', He put into our
lips the petition that we should all most desire. We are told, too,
what He desires: 'Who will have all men to be saved, and to
come to the knowledge of the truth'; 'Go ye into all the world,
and preach the Gospel to every creature.' Shall we not by faith
claim that the thing that He most wishes to be done on earth *shall*
be done? 'Thy people shall be willing in the day of Thy power.'
'All power *is* given unto Me.'

Has not the Lord been opening the lands to the Gospel, and
making travel easy for the very purpose that all should hear of
His love? 'The harvest truly is plenteous, but the labourers are
few; pray ye therefore the Lord of the harvest, that He will send
forth labourers into His harvest.'

Seeing that in days of old, faith wrought such mighty wonders
and that we 'on whom the ends of the world are come' have the
same God – seeing that God has 'provided some better thing for
us, that they without us should not be made perfect', shall we not
ask great things? Can we ask anything less than that the Gospel
shall be given speedily 'to every creature'? Nothing less will
satisfy our Master. Believing prayer will lead to whole-hearted
action, and the Lord for our encouragement says, 'If two of you
shall agree on earth as touching anything that they shall ask, it shall
be done for them of My Father which is in heaven.'

How many of God's people will band themselves together
afresh to claim in faith and to labour for the spread of the Gospel
to 'every creature' in this generation? Believing, we shall 'rejoice
in the Lord and glory in the Holy One of Israel', and shall prove
for ourselves and before the world that 'there is nothing too hard for
the Lord' and that all things are possible to him that believeth'.

In Time of Danger

As My Father hath sent Me, even so send I you (John 20:21).

The present time [a time of hostility] seems opportune for considering the course that we missionaries should adopt in times of excitement and danger.

First, then, let me remind you of the importance of the command not to speak evil of dignities, but on the contrary to pray for those in authority. Such prayer should be public as well as private. Much may depend on the officials finding that Christianity promotes loyalty to the powers that be.

Secondly, we do well to recognize that we are not here as representatives of Western Powers, and that our duties do not correspond with theirs. We are here as witnesses and representatives of the Lord Jesus Christ. Once, disciples mistakenly would have called down fire from heaven to avenge the Master Himself; but He rebuked them. Again, one of His disciples drew his sword in His defence, but our Saviour said, 'Put up again thy sword into his place; for all they that take the sword, shall perish with the sword.'

Thirdly: should we leave our stations? There are several reasons against this course. (a) We are in our stations at God's command, and as His ambassadors, and have both promise of, and claim to, His protection. (b) We are continually encouraging our converts to brave persecution and suffer loss for Christ's sake. Years of teaching would not impress them as our conduct at such times may do. A time of danger is a grand opportunity of being an object lesson. (c) The moral effect upon the heathen will be the same as upon the converts. We are not told to flee through fear of *possible* persecution. If the Lord suffers us to be driven away, the responsibility will then rest with Him. At such times tell-tale faces will witness for our Master, and a holy joy in God is a far better protection than a revolver. But it may not always be deliverance. There is something better than protection; but the martyr's crown is prepared for few, and such are prepared for it.

Whose I am, and whom I serve (Acts 27:23).
The beloved of the LORD shall dwell in safety by Him
(Deuteronomy 33:12).

The words, with which we commence this short paper, 'Possessed and Beloved', embody thoughts that are increasingly precious to us. When the Apostle was nearing shipwreck his heart relied on the truth that he was God's possession, as well as God's servant; and long before his day, the assurance given to his ancestor that 'the Beloved of the Lord shall dwell in safety by Him', had conveyed rest and confidence to many an Israelite indeed. Shall we not all rest in the same blessed fact? His by creation, His by redemption, we have again and again yielded ourselves to Him by our own glad consecration. *We* value and take care of our own possessions; *we* cherish and protect our beloved ones: how much more does *He*, whose love and whose resources so infinitely exceed ours!

As we review the mercies of the past we can say, 'We fasted and besought our God for this, and He *was* entreated of us.' But our needs are far greater today than ever before, and we earnestly desire the fervent prayers of our friends that guidance and help may be vouchsafed. The work is His; the workers are His; and His resources are pledged to supply every need. Yet for this He will be enquired of: believing prayer opens the very windows of heaven.

God's love hath hitherto sustained and blessed us; it is unchanging, because He is unchanging. We know not what the future may bring with it, but we know Him Who is the same yesterday, today and for ever. We put our hand afresh in His and say, 'Lead Thou me on.' Soon the Master may come; or if He tarry, one and another on whom we have learned to lean may be called away from our side; but '*Thou remainest*' – the great Rock-foundation which alone cannot be shaken. 'Because Thou hast been my help, therefore in the shadow of Thy wings will I rejoice.'

The Written Word

> If ye abide in Me, and My words abide in you, ye shall ask
> what ye will, and it shall be done unto you (John 15:7).

It is noteworthy that our Saviour does not say, 'Abide in Me, and
I in you', but, 'If ye abide in Me and *My words* abide in you'.
The substitution of 'My Words', for the 'I' in verse 4, brings out
the close connection between the Incarnate and the written Word.
To us Christ comes in the written Word, brought home to the
soul by the Holy Spirit. As we feed upon the written Word, we
feed upon the living Christ.

We *must* take time to be holy. It is not so much the quantity
of Scripture we read, as the subjects for meditation which we
find in it, that measure the nourishment we gain. On the other
hand our reading must not be too limited; for as the whole Paschal
Lamb was to be eaten, so the whole Word of God is profitable
and necessary 'that the man of God may be perfect, thoroughly
furnished unto all good works'. We would earnestly recommend
the consecutive reading of the whole Word of God to all who do
not so read it; and to all who are able to do so that the whole
Bible be read over in the course of the year. Where this cannot be
done prayerfully and thoughtfully, rather let a shorter portion be
taken for daily reading, still going through the whole of the Word
consecutively.

The verse before us shows the important connection existing
between a full knowledge of the Word of God and successful
prayer. Those prayers only will be answered which are in
harmony with the revealed will of God. Many of us have heard
earnest, but ignorant, believers praying for things clearly
contrary to the revealed purposes of God. Again a full knowledge
of the Word will often bring to our recollection appropriate
promises, and thus enable us to pray with faith and confidence.

Abiding in Christ and feeding upon His Word will lead to a
Christ-like walk, which will assure our hearts before God.

He Abideth Faithful

Is thy God, whom thou servest continually, able? (Daniel 6:20).

In every age, unbelief with a lamentable voice asks, as did Darius, this question, and in every age it has been the privilege of God's witnesses to give triumphant reply.

The very existence of the China Inland Mission is a standing testimony, more forcible than words, to God's faithfulness in answer to prayer. The Mission was born of prayer, nourished by prayer, and is still sustained month by month only in answer to believing prayer.

In the formation of the Mission it was seen that the divine plan to obtain labourers was to pray the Lord of the Harvest to thrust them forth. As we have needed workers we have done this, and workers have been given not merely from England, Scotland, Ireland and Wales but also from Norway, Sweden and Finland, from Denmark and Germany, Switzerland and Italy, from the United States and Canada, and from Australasia.

As to Funds. We saw long ago that we had the divine warrant to go forward in the Lord's work resting on His words: 'Seek ye first the Kingdom of God, and His righteousness, and all these things shall be added unto you.' And today we rest upon this promise and are not disappointed. We do not publish donors' names, we make no collections, we have no reserve funds, we never go into debt; our path now is as much walking on the waters as it was at the beginning. Have we not great cause to praise God?

And as to Open Doors, we have not been disappointed. He who holds the key of David, who opens and no man shuts, has set before us open doors all over China.

But the best remains to be told. All the foregoing continuous answers to prayer are but a means to the great end – *the salvation of souls*, and the furtherance of God's Kingdom. When we realize the value of one precious soul, what praise and thanks can we give to Him for the many thousands who are now witnessing, and in many cases suffering for Him?

Rock Foundations

> Everyone therefore which heareth these words of Mine, and doeth them, shall be likened to a wise man, which built his house upon the rock (Matthew 7:24).

It may be useful to recall, with thanksgiving, some of the precious truths on which the Lord founded the China Inland Mission. They are rock-foundations.

1. And first, the glorious truth that God *is* – that the Father *is*; that the Son *is*; that the Holy Spirit *is*; and that the blessed Triune God is the Rewarder of them that seek Him.

2. Again, that God *hath spoken*; that the Bible, the whole Bible, is the very Word of the living God.

3. That there is salvation in no other Name than that of Jesus Christ, the Crucified and Raised One.

4. That He, our risen Lord, has commanded that His Gospel shall be preached in all the world, and to every creature.

5. That all power has been given to Him in heaven and on earth – power over all flesh – and relying on His power and resources we are to go forth, counting on the Father's love.

6. That the Hope of the Church and the Hope for the world is the coming again of our Lord; and that we may hasten His coming by the proclamation of the Gospel.

7. That as many as have put on Christ are all one in Christ Jesus – equally bound to obey Him; equally heirs of His promises.

Acting on these principles, and in obedience to the Lord's commands, we have from the commencement invited the co-operation of God's people, without restriction as to denomination or nationality. The first band, the *Lammermuir* party, was international as well as inter-denominational, and now all Europe, with the exception of Belgium and Holland, are represented among us, also North America and Australasia. Is not this the Lord's doing, and is it not full of significance? We can say with Joshua: 'Not *one* thing hath failed of all the good things which the Lord your God spake.'

Go ye into all the world, and preach the Gospel to every creature
(Mark 16:15).

I do want to leave you with the thought that this is a very solemn
and very difficult work. I was reading over, only the other day,
some words of dear Hessie Newcombe, who laid down her life in
Kuch'eng – one whom I knew and loved much in the Lord, and
who was at our Mission house in Shanghai the year that she laid
down her life. 'What have we to face in China?' was the question
asked; and she sums all up in two short words: 'God and the
devil.' She speaks of what a solemn thing it is to be brought face to
face with the great enemy of souls, and to know all the time that
you are sitting, as it were, over a volcano which, apart from
God's restraining power, may burst forth at any moment. Were
they not prophetic words? God withdrew the restraint, and she and
her fellow-workers were honoured with the crown of martyrdom.

And this may take place anywhere in China, aye, in any
heathen country, if God should withdraw His restraining hand.
There are elements in India of very great danger. It appears to
me that we need to pray very much that God will keep them from
bursting forth. These are times of great danger in Africa. We
need to pray God to restrain the danger there, and protect His people.
I do trust that we shall all be in a prayerful spirit, remembering
that now, it may be, some of the Lord's servants in some parts of
China are in extreme danger, and are needing the support that our
prayers and sympathy may draw down from the Throne of Grace.

Rejectors of the Gospel are not to be found among the heathen
only. Oh, how many such there are to be found at home! And it
is a striking fact how many God is pleased to take to the ends of
the earth, and there save them by the selfsame Gospel that they
heard in the homeland without interest. Pray that the lives of all
missionaries in heathen lands, who come into contact with our
own countrymen, may be made mighty through God to bring
blessing to them.

God is able to make all grace abound unto you; that ye, having
all sufficiency in everything, may abound unto every good work
(2 Corinthians 9:8).

We are face to face with a very serious matter. Since the Chino-
Japanese war [1894] a totally new state of things has come in.
Taxation in China is very seriously increased, and the relative
value of silver and of various expenses has been very seriously
altered. This has been a source of some embarrassment. Where
work has been commenced on the ground that we had the funds
in hand, we have found that the funds have altered their value
before the work was completed.

Well, I need not tell you that in every case we had recourse –
may I say it reverently? – to our Great Treasurer, the Lord
Himself; and He has not failed us, and never will fail us, though
the expense of living in China is increasing considerably, and
the number to be supplied is increasing also. The great resources
of our great God are undiminished, and we rest upon them with
a full assurance that His word is as true now as it has ever been.
Our business is to 'seek first the Kingdom of God and His
righteousness, and all these things shall be added unto us'.

Time would fail me to dwell upon the instances which God
has given of His faithfulness, and I would encourage you and
encourage my own heart to trust in the faithful God, and not to
be afraid to go on praying the Lord of the harvest to send out
more labourers. I like to think of Him who sent three millions
of Israelites to bed without a crumb in the cupboard for breakfast
the next morning, and to remember they never got up in the
morning and found no breakfast ready to be gathered.

Oh! it is a great delight to me to feel that this is God's work.
Is it not so to you, dear friends? It is a great delight to feel that
we have a great and glorious God to deal with, and One who loves
to supply His people's need, and to show Himself strong on behalf
of those who put their trust in Him before the sons of men.

What is Faith?

Have faith in God (Mark 11:22).

I suppose there are very few children of God who have not often felt a great deal of difficulty with respect to this matter of faith; and I think that many times some of us – if one may speak for others – have felt a great deal of unnecessary difficulty about it, as though there was something mysterious in it.

What is faith? Is it not simply the recognition of the reliability or the trustworthiness of those with whom we have to do? Why do we accept with confidence a Government bond? Because we believe in the reliability of the Government. Men do not hesitate to put faith in the Government securities, because they believe in the Government that guarantees them. Why do we, without hesitation, put coins into circulation instead of, as in China, getting a lump of silver weighed and its purity investigated, before we can negotiate any money transaction with it? Because the Government issues the coin we use, and we use it with confidence and without difficulty. Why do we take a railway guide and arrange for a particular journey, or even, as I am doing, arrange for a journey which will extend for many months, and include Tasmania, New Zealand and America? Well, one has confidence in the reliability of these official publications. As a rule we are not put to shame!

Now, just as we use a railway guide we must use our Bible. We must depend on God's word just as we depend on man's word, only remembering that though man may not be able to carry out his promise, God will always fulfil what He has said. We must exercise the same confidence towards God as towards one another. Without confidence in one another the business and the commerce of the world would be impossible. Confidence in God is equally indispensable.

There are two sides of faith. There is the Godward side, and there is the manward side. It is when God's faithfulness is fully recognized by us that we shall be enabled to rest in quiet confidence and faith that He will fulfil His word.

If thou forbear to deliver them that are drawn unto death, and those that are ready to be slain; if thou sayest, Behold, we knew it not; doth not He that pondereth the heart consider it? and He that keepeth thy soul, doth not He know it? and shall not He render

to every man according to his works? (Proverbs 24:11-12).

Surely the claims of an empire like this should be not only admitted, but realized. Shall not the eternal interests of one-third of our race stir the deepest sympathies of our nature, the most strenuous efforts of our blood-bought powers? Shall not the low wail of helpless, hopeless misery, arising from half the heathen world, pierce our sluggish ears, and rouse us – body, soul and spirit – to one mighty, continued, unconquerable effort for China's salvation; that, strong in God's strength, and in the power of His might, we may snatch the prey from the hand of the mighty, may pluck these brands from the everlasting burnings, and rescue these captives from the thraldom of sin and Satan, to grace the triumphs of our sovereign King?

It is the prayerful consideration of these facts, and the deepening realization of China's awful destitution of all that can make man truly happy, that constrain the writer, by every means in his power, to lay its claims as a heavy burden upon the hearts of those who have already experienced the power of the blood of Christ; and to seek from the Lord the men and the means to carry the Gospel into every province of this benighted land. We have to do with Him who is the Lord of all power and might, whose arm is not shortened that it cannot save, whose unchanging word directs us to ask and receive, that our joy may be full; to open our mouths wide, that He may fill them. And we do well to remember that this gracious God, who has condescended to place His almighty power at the command of believing prayer, looks not lightly upon the blood-guiltiness of those who neglect to avail themselves of it for the benefit of the perishing.

PART 4

THE EVER-PRESENT LEADER

Himself hath said [to Joshua], I will never give thee up; I will never, never desert thee (Hebrews 13:5).

'A divine watchword for the new life.... In the word spoken to Joshua, and to all appearances spoken to him personally and alone (see Joshua 1:5), we are led equally to see a message from the heart of God straight to every Christian soul. Seldom, if ever, are we more powerfully and tenderly encouraged than we are here, to use with confidence that old-fashioned and now often disparaged sort of Bible study, the collection of eternal and universal principles of spiritual life out of an isolated text' (Bishop Handley Moule).

The Ever-present Leader

Jesus Christ is the same yesterday and today, yea and for ever
(Hebrews 13:8).

The wealth and fitness of the sequence here strikes one almost
with awe and amazement. Yet nothing less would have been
adequate. Among sentences which at first sight seem disjointed,
the continuity of thought is perfect. 'Remember your former
leaders', is the charge given in verse 7. 'Be not carried away by
divers and strange teaching', is the admonition of verse 9. On
the one hand stands sacred Tradition with its command that we
imitate the faith of the past. On the other hand stands Revolution
with its demand for change and experiment. Right in between
these two extremes is the great trumpet-call – the only call
sufficient for the situation, namely that 'Jesus Christ is the same
yesterday and today, yea and for ever'.

The past is not enough however good it be. Reverence for
the dead, strict adherence to tradition, can quickly develop into
a lifeless traditionalism, or a fruitless imitation, devoid of all
value. The past alone will not suffice. But though the under-
shepherds pass away, the Great Shepherd of the sheep – the Chief
Shepherd, as Peter calls Him – abides. The earthly leaders fall in
battle, but the Captain of the Lord's Host leads on. The faithful
Founder dies; but the Author and the Finisher of Faith remains.
The prophets spoke the message; but Christ the Word is in our
midst. Jesus Christ who was the inspiration of the past is the
same today, and is with us all the days.

Again, as the past is not enough for today, neither will it
suffice for tomorrow. Circumstances change, time advances,
'variegated and alien teachings' invade each new day. The
remembrance of former leaders, however devoted, will not save
us here. The arguments for innovations are specious and many.
'That which is old and waxed aged is nigh unto vanishing away',
is a truth few would deny. The past, however great, is now past

history. Tradition, however honourable, is merely tradition. Memory, however tenacious, is only memory. We may admire the retrospect, but we cannot live by it. We can feel the inspiration of the noble examples of yesterday, but the spirit that quickened them must quicken us. We look back, it is true, to the great cloud of witnesses; but they are only witnesses. We must 'look away unto' (ἀφορῶντες) Jesus, the Author and Perfector of our faith.

The great theme of the Epistle to the Hebrews – a message for all time – is the contrast between the transitory nature of the old dispensation and the absolute permanence of Christ and His finished work. The fathers and the prophets, though God spoke through them, pass away; but the Sun in whom now He speaks remains. The heavens perish, but Christ abides; they wax old as doth a garment, but He is the same and His years change not. Moses and others were faithful as servants, but Christ is the Son. In whatever light the old be regarded, Christ remains the substance of every type and shadow. He is the same yesterday and today, yea and for ever. 'Over the glory of His Being passes no shadow of turning. Never to the endless ages shall He need to be other than He is, or to be succeeded by a greater.' He is for ever the Alpha and the Omega.

Professor Gwatkin, in a striking passage in one of his books, has called attention to the way Christ has commanded history. 'Four times,' he says, 'in four distant ages the truth of Christ has had to be defended from a great and deadly enemy inside His Church. Every time the Spirit of Christ has pointed away from a church entangled in traditionalism to the living voice of Scripture; and each time fresh strength has come from a fresh revelation of the ever-living Person of whom Scripture speaks. The first of these crises was the contest with Gnosticism, the second was with Arianism; the Reformation was the third; the fourth is the great scientific controversy opened by the Deists, which seems gathering to its hottest battle in our own time.'

Had Professor Gwatkin lived and written today he might have referred to the terrible assaults which now come from outside the Church. But wherever the danger lies, whether within or without, fresh strength can only come from a fresh realization of the ever-living Christ.

One of our modern historians has spoken of the great and vital periods of history, and then states that, 'there succeed dead ages that seem to do nothing but echo'. This cannot fail to be the experience of the Church if it only remembers the past and forgets the ever-living Christ. To read of and reverence the Jesus of History is not in itself enough; we must believe that He is still the same today. It is of course essential that we should at all times recall what He did for us in the days of His flesh; but for today's problems we need not only a Christ who died, but a Christ who ever lives, a Christ for today, an eternal Christ.

Have we grasped in anything like a vital fashion the tremendously significant truth that Jesus Christ is the same today as yesterday. To have known Christ 'after the flesh' must have been an unspeakable privilege, but we are warned that that is insufficient and that there is something immeasurably greater. All the manifold differences between those days in Palestine and our own time sink into insignificance before the fact of His unchanging Presence. He is the great Contemporary of all time, of today as of yesterday, or yesterday as of tomorrow. Do we live, do we act, do we think, as though He were really with us now? Yet we cannot be what we should be on any other supposition. 'He Himself hath said, I will in no wise fail thee, neither will I in any wise forsake thee.' He is with us as He was with Paul, and as He was with Hudson Taylor, the same, the ever-unchanging Christ.

The permanent value of Hudson Taylor's life and message is just this, that what Jesus Christ was to him yesterday He will be to us today. If the laws of nature changed we could not rely upon the findings of Newton and other men of science, and if spiritual truth changed, the past would have no lessons for us. As we see what God has been to one of His servants we know what He will be to us today and tomorrow. Christ is the ever-flowing Spring from whom we may at all times draw a fresh supply.

We commemorate not that we may exalt the man, but that we may be stimulated to imitate his faith. We commemorate that we may give God the glory. 'Let Jesus wear the crown,' sang Bunyan's Christian. And the same song shall be ours. 'He that glorieth, let him glory in the Lord.' The vital element in Hudson Taylor's legacy is not what he was, but that to which he bore witness. He was a witness-bearer, by word and by life, to the great fact that 'God is faithful, through whom' both he and we 'were called into the fellowship of His Son Jesus Christ our Lord'.

1st Day

God's Guardian Care

The LORD is my Shepherd; I shall not want (Psalm 23:1).

It is the will of our Father that His children shall be absolutely without carefulness. 'Be careful for nothing' is as definite a requirement as 'Thou shalt not steal.' To enable us, however, to carry out this command, we need to *know* the constancy of His solitude who ever careth for us; and we need to make use of the direction. 'In everything, by prayer and supplication, with thanksgiving, let your requests be made known unto God.'

The comfort of this blessed assurance is the happy portion of all the people of God; of our friends and supporters at home, equally with our toiling labourers abroad.

What a comfort it is to notice how largely the indicative mood is used in the Scriptures. In the present Psalm, for instance, we find the subjunctive mood only in one clause of the fourth verse. All the definiteness and assurance we can desire are conveyed by positive affirmations in the indicative mood; and it is noteworthy that each encouragement is either conveyed in the present tense, or is based upon it: 'The LORD is my Shepherd; I *shall* not want.'

It is cheering to remember that for the sake of His own Name, and of His own glory, as well as for the sake of His great love, the full supply of all our needs is guaranteed by our relationship to Him as our Shepherd. A lean, scraggy sheep with torn limbs and tattered fleece would be small credit to the shepherd's care; but unless we *will* wander from Him, and *will not* remain restfully under His protection, there is no fear of such ever being our lot.

'The LORD is my Shepherd.' He saith not *was*; He saith not *may be*, or *will be*. 'The LORD *is* my Shepherd' – *is* on Sunday, *is* on Monday, and *is* through every day of the week; *is* in January, and *is* in December, and in every month of the year; *is* at home, and *is* in China; *is* in peace and *is* in war; in abundance and in penury. Let us live in the joy of this truth.

Rest in Service

> He maketh me to lie down in pastures of green grass: He
> leadeth me beside the waters of quietness (Psalm 23:2).

Soothing, tranquillizing words, of living, loving power! As we read them, a feeling of restfulness comes over the weary, way-worn heart. The very mention of pastures of tender grass and trickling streams is refreshing.

The first words of the first verse – The LORD – are the key to the whole Psalm, a key which, if fully grasped, would make life itself a psalm. And just so it is in this verse: the first word in each clause, 'He', gives to the precious words their sweetness and their power.

The longer we meditate on these God-given words, the more full of meaning do we find them and more appropriate do they appear. The lying down suggests such sweet rest; and not merely rest, but satisfaction; for a hungry, unsatisfied sheep would need to feed and not to lie down. And oh! the depth of the preciousness of the words, 'He maketh me to lie down.' Do we not know all too well what it is to be too weary to lie down – too restless to be able to take the needed quiet. But when He giveth quietness, who then can make trouble? When He maketh us to lie down, who can harass and distress?

But what when fiery trials threaten to consume us? Ah, there too our Shepherd is at work. It is common in many parts of China for the herbage to become so rank, and dry, and coarse and full of vermin as to become a source of danger. Then the shepherd leads his flock to a place of security while he sets fire to the hillsides. And a beautiful sight it is. But the scene changes; the storm becomes a calm, and as by magic, a beautiful carpet of living green covers hill and dale. Not unneeded was the scorching fire, nor in vain did the storm burst; the issue is seen in the soft, quiet beauty and the rich fertility that follow.

Faith, however, needs not to see; she foresees and rejoices even while the storm lasts, well assured of the blessings.

God's Gracious Leadings

> He restoreth my soul: He leadeth me in the paths of
> righteousness for His name's sake (Psalm 23:3).

The word here rendered 'restoreth', suggests to the mind of the English reader the restoration of a wanderer. This, however, is not the primary idea of the word used in the original. It is rather restoration from depression or exhaustion that is indicated. The same word in Psalm 19:7 is rendered 'converting' – 'The law of the Lord is perfect, converting the soul'; that is, restoring the cheerful tone of the soul when depressed by calamity, or when wearied by service.

Viewed in this light, this verse suggests two most comforting thoughts: (1) *Fresh* supplies of strength, *fresh* supplies of grace and of Christian joy, as the exigencies of service may require; and (2) leading, guidance – guidance in right paths; than which no assurances could be more encouraging. And then, coupled with these two grounds of encouragement, we have the gracious assurance that He does this for His own Name's sake. It is not for *His* glory that His service should be, or should appear to be, a toilsome slavery, wearing out the life and the joy of those engaged in it. On the contrary, the Lord's people should always, with tell-tale faces, be unconsciously proclaiming that His service is a service of freedom, that the joy of the Lord is their strength, that He leads His own by right paths, and that He glorifies His own great Name in them, and through them continually. May the Lord give us all the joy of *realizing* that for His own Name's sake, that for His own credit's sake, He will renew our strength as we wait upon Him; He will guide us during the whole pilgrim-life with His own infallible counsel, and then, when He has glorified Himself in us, will bring us safely to His own glory at last.

Those who pray, and those who give at home, and those who toil abroad, are associated together; and in their corporate capacity they may take the full comfort which the assurances of this precious verse are well calculated to convey.

Yea, though I walk through the valley of the shadow of death, I will fear no evil; for Thou art with me; Thy rod and Thy staff they comfort me (Psalm 23:4).

The Good Shepherd – oh, how good! *Our* Lord and *our* Shepherd! As we have seen, all concerning Him and His ways has been definite and sure – in the indicative mood; has been instant and constant – in the ever-present tense. Why are we so prone to turn our eyes from Him and His glorious immutability to our ever-changing selves and our subjunctive moods, our ifs, our thoughts, our perhapses?

'Yea, though I walk through the valley of the shadow of death.' Here comes in the subjunctive mood: here, and here only. It is not said, 'I *shall* walk through the valley.' It may be that our present heaven of communion with the Living, Loving One shall soon and suddenly be swallowed up in the glories of His appearing! But if not, what then? Shall we be left in the dark to tremble with fear? Shall we be left alone in unaided conflict with the powers of darkness? 'I will fear no evil for Thou art with me.' 'Thou *art* with me.' There is no subjunctive here. 'Thy rod and Thy staff' – the badges of the shepherd's office, the warrants of the security of the sheep – they are my comfort, they are my stay.

Timid hearts sometimes misread these symbols, and take the Shepherd's rod as the rod of chastening; but while chastening has its place in Scripture, it is never found in connection with the figures of the Shepherd and His flock, or the Lawgiver and His people. The rod of Moses became a sign to Pharaoh. It brought judgment on God's enemies; but it brought no chastening to Israel. By it the Red Sea was divided, for deliverance to them; and by it the waters were brought back again, for the final destruction of the armies of Egypt. We may well thank God for the Shepherd's rod.

More tender and more touching is the Shepherd's staff. It tells of One who was willing to become a Pilgrim, not untouched with the feelings of our infirmities. 'Thy rod and Thy staff they comfort me.'

Royal Supplies

Thou preparest a table before me in the presence of mine enemies:
Thou anointest my head with oil; my cup runneth over
(Psalm 23:5).

Pleasant as are the pastures of tender grass, and refreshing as
are the sparkling brooklets, to which the Good Shepherd often
leads His flock, there are graces and virtues of the believer which
must be developed in a sterner school: every true disciple shall
be perfected as His Master, and when he is tried he shall come
forth as gold.

It would be a great mistake, however, to suppose that the discipline of warfare even is all painful. The joys of victory are not
greater than the joys of faith – a faith that rests and delights itself
in the living God, and glories in Him as much before the conflict has begun as it rejoices in Him when the victory is achieved.

'Thou preparest a table before me in the *presence* of mine
enemies.' Was there no joy in the hearts of Caleb and Joshua
when they triumphantly declared of the dreaded foes: 'They are
bread for us: their defence is departed from them'? Was Jonathan
troubled in the presence of his enemies when he exclaimed: 'There
is no restraint to the Lord to save by many or by few'? What
were David's feelings when he said: 'Who is this uncircumcised
Philistine, that he should defy the armies of the living God'?
Oftentimes have the armies of the Lord of Hosts gone forth to
war as did Jehoshaphat, who appointed singers to go before the
army, praising the Lord, whose mercy endureth for ever! Rich
spoils are gathered when the people of God battle after that sort!

We cannot fail to see how much richer are the blessings
mentioned in the latter half of this Psalm than those of the former.
It is in the valley of the shadow of death that solid, Divine comforts
are brought to light. But this is not all. The conflict terminates,
the darkness passes away; but the spoils are permanent, and the
gains are eternal.

Unlimited Blessing

Surely goodness and mercy shall follow me all the days of my
life; and I shall dwell in the house of the LORD for ever
(Psalm 23:6).

A fitting ending this to a Psalm beginning with the LORD –
JEHOVAH! Let us only see to it that He is in His right place –
first and foremost – and that His name is ever printed in large
capitals on our hearts and in our lives – while all that appertains
to us follows, and follows in small type – and then our life service
will begin to be glorious, it will continue to be increasingly
blessed and successful, and its end will be triumphant!

How can it be that Christian life is so often felt, and confessed,
to be a comparative failure, while there is such encouragement
and help? Is it not that this mistake mars it all, that we are *not*
really making Him our Lord – our first thought – our ruling
consideration? Ourselves, our interests, our families, practically
stand before Him: we gladly give to Him that which will not
interfere with our life-plans, our enjoyments, or the supposed
interests or pleasures of those dear to us. There can be no true
rest and fullest happiness while this is the case.

Far otherwise is the life that accords with this beautiful Psalm!
The Lord first – the Lord as the Owner, the Ruler, the Provider,
the Guide – and all fear of want and all fear of failure are gone.
We are enabled to lie down in pastures of tender grass; we are
led by waters of quietness. Restored and refreshed when faint
and weary, we are kept in and led by paths of righteousness, for
His Name's sake. Is faith to be proved, and approved, in dark
and trying paths? Consciously the Lord's, we fear no evil, and
safely follow whither He doth lead. His rod and His staff are our
comfort and our stay; nay, more – in the presence of our enemies
He prepares the royal feast. All the days of our life we are thus
attended; and at last, in the many mansions of the Father's home,
we shall dwell in the house of the Lord for ever!

Him hath God exalted with His right hand to be a Prince and a
Saviour, for to give repentance to Israel, and forgiveness of sins
(Acts 5:31).

The words quoted above indicate the offices to which Christ is
raised by God. Let us mark well the order; you must accept the
Prince if you would receive the Saviour. Many wish they were
saved, and remain unconverted, because they do not give up
themselves, their wills, their all, to God. Many, again, are only
half saved, because they do not accept the Prince for this life,
and consequently have no Saviour to deliver them effectively
in the hour of temptation. They see their life pictured as they
watch some little child trying to walk; it can creep, but when it
tries to walk it stumbles and falls. So it is with kingless lives.
Oh, it does not pay to refuse the King! As the prodigal starved
and was clothed with rags while the Father's house had the best
robe waiting and the fatted calf, so there is rest, there is peace
and joy, there is fruitfulness and power *inside* the Kingdom.

Is it so with you, my reader? Do you prosper in all you
undertake? Are all your prayers answered? Does each morning
bring you no fear? Is each day a psalm, each night a thanksgiving,
sometimes sung in the minor key – but still sung? Does your
servant, as she goes into the kitchen, see the witness of the
Kingdom there? Does He reign in the wardrobe? Do your visitors
feel impressed with the reality of the Kingdom? Or, are there
many things, some things, perhaps only one little thing, about
which you claim to decide for yourself? Remember, that only
one such claim dethrones altogether your Lord and Master, so
far as lies in your power, no matter how trivial the matter may
be. It says: 'I will not have this Man to reign over me.' If you
were living or meant to live in accordance with His will, you
would be only too glad to let Him be King, and to take in all His
fulness, as you gave Him all your weakness and failure. Is He
King to you when He says: 'Go ye into all the world; and preach
the Gospel to every creature'?

The Prince of Peace

His Name shall be called Wonderful, Counsellor, Mighty God, Everlasting Father, Prince of Peace (Isaiah 9:6).

One of the titles given to our Lord in the prophecies of Isaiah is 'Wonderful', another is 'Counsellor'. The margin of the Revised Version, combining the two, reads, 'Wonderful Counsellor'. And truly He is wonderful in counsel and excellent in working. By ways very different from those which we could devise or execute, He trains His people in their service, and thus makes them to become meet and fit for the inheritance of the saints in light. Then, when they are fitted for it, when the last polish has been received and the last refinement has been gained, He takes away those whom we would fain retain to grace the Paradise above.

We know not for what He is preparing us, and consequently we cannot understand many of His dealings. But we can do what is better – we can trust Him. Triumphant faith – not merely submission to the will of God, but exulting delight in it, even when most crushing to flesh and blood – can *now* sing in anticipation, as we shall all sing soon together, 'Our Jesus hath done all things well'.

In the passage from Isaiah to which we have referred, the prophecy tells us that the government shall be upon the shoulders of the Wonderful Counsellor, whose name is also called The Prince of Peace. And it continues: 'Of the increase of His government and of peace there shall be no end'. First, He Himself is brought before us, then His government and its issues – peace, unending peace. How often we lack the peace because of want of hearty acceptance of Him and acquiescence in and co-operation with His government.

And yet that government is no harsh or arbitrary one. The hand that holds the sceptre is a pierced hand, and the shoulder on which it rests first bore for each one of us the heavy cross. Is it not safe to trust the government of One whose love has redeemed us at such a cost, and made us His own at the price of His blood?

Whence should we have so much bread in the wilderness, as to
fill so great a multitude? (Matthew 15:33).

This narrative brings us at the very outset, and keeps before us
all through, the presence of our blessed Lord. 'Jesus called His
disciples unto Him.' Jesus opened their hearts to the sympathy
and compassion of His own heart: 'I have compassion on the
multitude; I will not send them away fasting'. This is just what
we need: we want our dear Master to draw us near Himself; to
open His own heart to us. Then this narrative brings before us
the disciples of the Lord as the instruments through which He
wrought His greatest work. He would do nothing independently
of them, and I think there is a lesson for us to learn that we
should not work independently of one another. How closely should
we be knit together to do the work He has given us to do!

Then we have brought before us the multitude. I am so glad it
was a great multitude, and that the disciples thought it was
impossible to feed them. We are apt to be too arithmetical in
our thoughts. In the presence of our Lord it was no matter how
many there were. I have often thought it better to have small
resources, in the hand of God, who is able to multiply them, than
it is to have much. What God has given us is all we need: we
require nothing more. It is not a question of large supplies; it is
just a question of the presence of the Lord.

Let us look at the Lord's methods. How were the people fed?
By the united action of Christ and His disciples. He claimed their
all; they gladly gave up their all, and unhesitatingly obeyed all
His directions. If there had been some stingy arithmeticians there,
they might have set to work to calculate. It was not a question of
how many loaves; it was just a question of entire consecration.
Let us give up our work, our thoughts, our plans, ourselves, our
loved ones, our influence, our *all* right into His hand, and then
there will be nothing left to be troubled about. When all is in His
hand all will be safe, all will be done and well done.

The Blessing of God

And the LORD spake unto Moses, saying, Speak unto Aaron
and unto his sons, saying, On this wise ye shall bless the
children of Israel;... They shall put My Name upon the
children of Israel; and I will bless them (Numbers 6:22-27).

In the concluding verses of Numbers 6 we see one of the fullest
forms of benediction to be found in the whole Word of God. The
thought naturally arises: Why are they found here? The reply is
twofold. There is the Divine side. From God's heart of love first
came the privilege of Nazarite consecration; and then the act of
consecration calls forth His rich benedictions. On the human side
we may learn that the soul that is fully consecrated always receives
the blessing of God. Where that blessing is not enjoyed, there is
always something unreal or defective in the consecration.

How many Christians there are who, in their self-will and
attempted self-management, find themselves day by day full of
sorrow or full of care. Trying to keep themselves, they are not
kept; trying to be happy, they are often unhappy; trying to succeed,
they fail. But God delights to give His blessing to those who have
dedicated themselves and their all to Him. Note how spontaneous
and unsought is the blessing from God – the Lord *commanded*
Aaron and his sons to bless Israel, and to put His Name upon
them; and declares His unalterable purpose, 'I *will* bless them.'

What is the real meaning of blessing? We frequently use the
word so vaguely as to lose much of its preciousness. We use it as
a synonym of praise, but blessing does not mean praise, for God
blesses us. Sometimes we use it for some gracious gift, but
blessing does not signify gift. Blessing is the moving of the
heart toward an object of affection and complacency. The outgoing
of the heart is naturally accompanied by gift or ascription. When
our hearts bless the Lord in song, the blessing is not in the song,
but in the feeling that prompts it. When the Lord blesses His
people with peace and plenty, it is His heart that moves His loving
Hand.

The Blessing of the Father

The LORD bless thee, and keep thee: The LORD make His face shine upon thee, and be gracious unto thee: The LORD lift up His countenance upon thee, and give thee peace (Numbers 6:24-26).

In the light of the fuller revelation of the New Testament we can scarcely fail to see in this threefold benediction the blessing of the Father, of the Son, and of the Holy Spirit. So read, we see in the words fuller beauty and appropriateness. Let us take the first clause, then, as the Father's blessing.

Considered as a father's blessing could anything be more appropriate than 'The Lord bless thee, and keep thee'? Is it not just what every loving father seeks to do – to bless and keep his children? He does not find it an unwelcome task, but his greatest delight. Offer to relieve him of the responsibility and to adopt his child, and see what his reply will be! Nor may we confine ourselves to paternal love alone, but take it as embracing the love of the mother as well, for 'Thus saith the Lord;... As one whom his mother comforteth, so will I comfort you.' And we all know how the mother-love delights to lavish itself on the objects of its care. With a patience that never tires, and an endurance almost inexhaustible, and a care all but unlimited, how often has the mother sacrificed her very life for her babe. But strong as is a mother's love, it may fail; God's love never.

It was one of the objects of our Saviour's mission to reveal to us that, in Christ Jesus, God is our Father. How He delighted to bring out this precious truth the Sermon on the Mount bears witness.

And what a glorious Father He is! The source of all true fatherhood and motherhood. The sum of all human goodness, and tenderness, and love is but as the dew-drop to the sun. How safe too! Ofttimes where the love of earthly parents has not failed, yet have they been powerless to bless and keep. And it is an individual blessing: 'The Lord bless *thee*, and keep *thee*.' And it includes every form of blessing, temporal as well as spiritual.

The Blessing of the Son

The LORD bless thee, and keep thee: The LORD make His face shine upon thee, and be gracious unto thee: The LORD lift up His countenance upon thee, and give thee peace (Numbers 6:24-26).

We now come to the second blessing: the blessing of the Son. Through eternal ages the Son of God, He became, in fulness of time, the Son of Man. He came to manifest, as well as to speak of, the Father's love. Time would fail us to enumerate the acts of typical service fulfilled in Him.

'The Lord make His face shine upon thee.' The face is perhaps the most wonderful part of the wonderful human body. Of all the faces that God has made no two are exactly alike, even when quiescent; and though we do occasionally meet with those that bear a very close resemblance, intimate friends, who know the play of the countenance, never mistake. And why is this? Because God has so ordered it that the face shall reveal the character and feelings of the individual. And it is the purpose of God that the heart of Christ shall be revealed to His people. It is the will of God that 'the light of the knowledge of the glory of God' should be revealed to us 'in the face of Jesus Christ'.

Where there is the shining of the face we know there is more than forgiveness; there is favour. 'Cause Thy face to shine and we shall be saved.' What a wonderful view of the light of His countenance the favoured disciples must have had who were witnesses of His transfiguration! We are told His face did shine as the sun. To the proto-martyr Stephen the heavens were opened and the face of the Lord shone upon him: and when he saw Him he became so like Him that his dying utterances correspond to those of his Lord on the cross. When Saul, likewise, saw the glory of the risen Saviour, the vision at midday was of a light above the brightness of the sun; and the effect of that vision changed his whole life. And when the Lord makes the light of His countenance to shine upon any of His people, there is a moral and progressive change into His likeness.

The Blessing of the Spirit

The LORD bless thee, and keep thee: The LORD make His face shine upon thee, and be gracious unto thee: The LORD lift up His countenance upon thee, and give thee peace (Numbers 6:24-26).

The blessing of the Spirit is essential to the completeness of the benediction. We are struck, however, with the similarity of this blessing to that which preceded it; nor is this similarity surprising, for, as the Son came to reveal the Father, so the Spirit has come to reveal the Son. Christ was a true Comforter, and the Holy Spirit is the other Comforter, sent by the Father in Christ's name, that He might abide with the Church for ever. Christ is the indwelling Saviour; the Holy Spirit the indwelling Comforter. On whomsoever Christ makes His face to shine, the Holy Spirit will surely lift up His countenance.

'And give thee peace.' Are we practically enjoying this blessing? Are we finding that when He makes quietness, none can make trouble? And if not, why not?

We shall never forget the blessing we received through the words, 'Whosoever drinketh of the water I shall give him shall never thirst.' As we realized that Christ literally meant what He said – that 'shall' meant shall, and 'never' meant never, and 'thirst' meant thirst – our heart overflowed with joy as we accepted the gift. Oh, the thirst with which we sat down, but oh, the joy with which we sprang from our seat, praising the Lord that the thirsting days were all past, and past for ever! For, as our Lord continues: 'the water that I shall give Him shall be *in him* a well of water, springing up – overflowing – unto everlasting life'. Perhaps, however, we should draw attention to the words of Christ: 'whosoever drinketh' – not drank once for all – but 'drinketh', that is habitually. After promising that out of him 'shall flow rivers of living water', it is added: 'this spake He of the Spirit, which they that believe' – *i.e.* keep believing – were to receive. It is intended for each one – 'and give *thee* peace.' Would that each reader would accept the gift *now*.

> And they shall put My Name upon the children of Israel;
> and I will bless them (Numbers 6:7).

With these words the great object of God in bestowing His blessing upon His people is revealed: 'they shall put My Name upon the children of Israel', or in other words shall cause them to become the people of God.

In olden times names were not meaningless, but were descriptive of character or relationship. The various names of God are all full of significance, and each is always used designedly in the Bible: failing to recognize this, spiritually-ignorant men have imagined the Old Testament writings to have been mere compilations from the works of different authors, and have failed to see the beautiful appropriateness of the various names of God as they are used in different connections.

The thrice-repeated Name of Jehovah has revealed to us the triune God in His gracious relations with His redeemed people, and has reminded us that in these relationships He is the unchanging One, the same yesterday, today and for ever. Israel of old was, and still is, God's witness in the world. In all their unfaithfulness, their very existence as a separate people is a standing miracle, witnessing to the truth of prophecy. We are now the children of God – Christians upon whom the Name of Christ has been called – and are intended to be witnesses for our Master. There is an interesting parallelism between this passage and the commission given by our Lord to His people to disciple all nations, baptizing them into the *Name* of the Father, the Son and the Holy Ghost.

The words, 'And I will bless them', are an encouragement to Aaron and his sons in pronouncing the blessing, as well as to the people who received it. The blessing was preceded by a command, and followed by a promise; even as our Saviour in giving His last commission to disciple all nations followed it by the assurance and promise, 'Lo, I am with you always'. In the word of a King there is power.

From a letter to his sister Amelia, dated September, 1854.

Thank God there is One to whose presence we ever have access and peculiar nearness, and for whose aid we can apply in every time of need. Trials we are not exempt from, and some of them are very painful and difficult to bear; but I shall feel amply repaid if one soul only – one precious never-dying soul – is, by my instrumentality, rescued from the powers of darkness and brought into the fold of Christ. But I trust that not one only, but many, will be turned to righteousness by the Word of God ministered by me.

Would you feel this a sufficient recompense for similar privations? Would you be willing to learn in a peculiar sense what it is to devote yourself to the service of God – to present yourself a living sacrifice, holy, acceptable to God, and consider it your reasonable service? Are you willing to exemplify your love to Jesus as greater than that you bear to father and mother, brethren and sisters, and houses and lands, by leaving your dear friends and beloved country for Jesus' sake, and in compliance with His command in Matthew 28:19-20? Then hearken to the Macedonian cry of China and come over and help us. Can you leave China's millions to perish unwarned, untaught, unaided, uncared for, and yet calmly enjoy your own privileges? Take this matter to the Throne of Grace; weigh the subject in the light of eternity.

Oh! were it at the expense of every source of earthly enjoyment; were health and peace, and comfort and happiness, and even life itself, to be sacrificed that we might communicate the blessings of Christianity to others, we ought gladly to make it. But there is no surer way of finding happiness than by heartily engaging in the work of the Lord; no more certain ways of increasing our own blessings than by endeavouring to communicate them to others; and these are not only means of obtaining happiness, but are themselves the highest and purest enjoyments we are capable of receiving. Oh! for eloquence to plead the cause of China; for a pencil dipped in fire to paint the condition of this people!

16th Day

From a letter, dated July 1855, to a bereaved Uncle.

There are times when one feels most acutely what it is to be separated by 18,000 miles from all that is dear and beloved in this world, and perhaps I may say that my position does in some measure enable me to feel more true sympathy for you; for here we feel what it is to be deprived of the society and friendship and aid of those we love. My position – one of peculiar loneliness and isolation – has let me feel something of the desolation which you have doubtless experienced....

Doubtless you too, dear Uncle, have found that while passing through the deep waters He has been with you, and while passing through the furnace He has not forsaken you, for 'faithful is He that promised'. It is often when the world seems most desolate, and our hearts are bleeding under the loss of all that we prized, when all around us seems gloom and before us darkness, when the spirit is subdued with sorrow and longs to enter into its rest – then it often is that 'the still small voice' is heard whispering with melting tenderness: 'I am thy portion and thy exceeding great reward'. Then, too, is the time when we can appreciate a portion which changeth not and shall never pass away.

How incomprehensible is the love of God! His ways are indeed past finding out. How many of His provinces are like the cloud between the Israelites and the Egyptians – if looked on by unbelievers, or without faith, it is a cloud of darkness; but if viewed according to the privilege of the Lord's people, it is no longer darkness but light and safety. May this be your experience; may you feel that the Hand which inflicts the wound supplies the balm; and that He who has emptied your heart has filled the void with Himself.

How painful is the death of those we love! I was much struck with this thought this morning, when preaching from John 3:16, to my little congregation of Chinese. God so loved us, that He spared not His only-begotten Son that we might inherit unending bliss!

17th Day

The Prodigal Son

From a letter to a Backslider, dated 1855.

On preparing to write, memory darts back and presents in most lively fashion bygone times when we were together – the class-meetings we used to attend, the prayer-meetings in which we both engaged, the conversations on religious subjects we held; then our meetings around the piano are so vividly portrayed, that it would be in vain to attempt to describe the feelings they give rise to.

I do not forget you at the Throne of Grace. I have often looked with regret while I saw you wandering from the fold – the true fold, the only fold, in this barren wilderness, and I thank God that you have found it to be thus and look back to the time when all was freedom, safety, joy and peace: when the gentle Shepherd of Israel led you beside the still waters. You have wandered from your Best Friend, but *He* has not ceased to care for you. He has followed you, and while allowing you to feel where you were, His love has been ceaselessly employed in providing you with blessings, and preserving you from evil of which you were unconscious.

Turn again; say with the Prodigal Son, 'I will arise and will go to *my Father*, and will say, Father, I have sinned, and am not worthy to be called Thy son', and while you are afar off our Father will run and meet you. He who upbraideth not will change your ragged garments for the perfect, glorious, imperishable robe of Christ's righteousness....

It is very important to have clear views of the plan of salvation, not to confuse the finished work of Christ with His present work and the operations of the Spirit. The work of Atonement is a finished work; it was finished on Calvary, and there Jesus bore all the sins of all the world – past, present and future. His resurrection declared with power the truth of the 'It is finished' Jesus Himself proclaimed as He laid down His life.... Without any loss of time, while reading this letter, take the place of the sinner and say: 'Father I have sinned; forgive me for Jesus' sake, according to Thy promise.'

The Plan of Salvation

From the same letter as on the previous page.

Our sins are atoned for, whether I am a Christian, an infidel, or heathen; whether I believe it or not. My condemnation now is not that I am a sinner – for who is not? – but that light is come into the world and I love darkness rather than light. What then must I do to be saved? 'Believe on the Lord Jesus Christ.' He that believeth on the Son hath eternal life – is passed from death unto life. If I fear my sins are too heavy to be forgiven, I lose sight of the fact that they are and have been perfectly atoned for. If I doubt the willingness of God to pardon me, I make Him a liar, for His Word says, 'If we confess our sins, He is faithful and just to forgive us our sins.' It is not 'He is willing', but 'He is faithful and just', and why? Because our debt has been borne; it would be unfaithful and unjust to recharge it if we confess our sins. That is our part.

But if I say: 'I believe all this, but I don't feel miserable enough about my sins.' Is it my feelings or Christ's Atonement I have to look at? What I have to do is simply, just as I am, without any further preparation, to take the place of the sinner. Having confessed my sin and pleaded the Atonement of Jesus, I know God is faithful and just to forgive my sins and to cleanse me from all unrighteousness.

He has also promised His Holy Spirit to those who ask It. I have asked It, and as He is faithful He will give me my desire. But if I think I don't feel this or that, I must remember that my salvation does not depend on feelings, but on faith. Feelings of sorrow for sin, joy in the pardon received, are the fruits of the Spirit, not the grounds of justification. Satan may tempt, but my anchor is fixed; here I remain.

Having received Christ, He gives me power to become the son of God, and to bring forth fruit. My pardon and acceptance rest only on the finished atonement of Jesus. Now He is my Mediator and Advocate. The fruits of the Spirit are the result of my being in Christ and receiving the gift of the Spirit.

The Lord's Vineyard

From a letter dated October 25, 1855, re. the need of workers.

This island (Tsung-ming) is some sixty to seventy miles long, by nearly twenty broad. Its population is between one and two million. With the exception of the visit of Mr. Burdon and myself, this island has been an untouched portion of the Lord's Vineyard.... May they not well say, 'No man careth for my soul'?

It is not my place to call labourers into the Lord's vineyard – this the Lord of the harvest alone can do. But is it a good sign to see among the thousands of Christians in England many willing to give a subscription to a Missionary Society, and then think they have done their duty?

There are millions of people and thousands of towns and villages accessible which have never been visited. The missionary visits some, never to return. Now, I appeal to you, are the people likely to believe the message, or to think that he merely came on a pleasure excursion? They will think, 'This is but a foreign doctrine of no importance!' In England many are Gospel-hardened, while here millions are perishing from lack of knowledge. Everyone ought, in the sight of God, to inquire, 'Am I justified in staying at home under these circumstances?' Many will say, 'But one ought to ask, Am I called to go?' – and very properly too, for it is a most important question – yet how few, on the other hand, take the command, 'Go ye into all the world', and ask, 'Am I justified in not going?'

I was much struck with the fact that, after the recent division among the Wesleyans [the Secession of 1848] – when so large a number of local preachers, leaders, and members left – the funds and the wants of the villages as to preachers were soon nearly all supplied. I know something as to how it was managed; but this conclusion forces itself on me: if men can do thus, suppose all these workers were drafted to some mission station, has the Lord no power to preserve the home-field from suffering loss? I commend this thought to you; you will only give it its value.

Looking to God Alone

From a letter, dated May 1856, to Benjamin Broomhall.

Do not forget the importance of walking according to the light you have, while seeking for more. If you feel you are called to the work, do not fear as to the way and the time. He will make all plain. The eye of faith looks to Jesus, and walks, in spite of winds and waves, on the water. I understand that the funds of the Society had somewhat fallen off a short time ago, on account, I suppose, of the war. But that does not affect me, as I have received from other sources funds for my own use and for various purposes, so that I have not needed to draw on the Society for some time, and have in hand what will probably supply me for six months to come. And only by the last mail I had a letter from a valued friend and devoted servant of Christ, who has sent me £100 within the last six months, pressing to know if there are any means of usefulness in which he can aid in supplying the means in addition to what I may now be able to do. So, as you truly say, if we are doing the will of God, no circumstances can hinder, no dangers prevent. Nothing can hinder or frustrate His designs....

I am sure you will excuse me if I press on you the importance of seeking from God guidance and direction for yourself personally, unconnected with the movements of others. Everyone has an individual duty to perform to God; the actings of others cannot make that duty other than it is; nor can the claims of duty be remitted me because of the course – right or wrong – of others. We may, and should, thank God for all the aid He gives us through others in the performance of duty; and let us endeavour to see our way clear, independently of others; and then, in any circumstances of trial or perplexity, we shall find the comfort of it, and not be leaning on an arm of flesh. The Lord bless and guide you, and give you ever to lean unshaken on His faithfulness!

The Only True Rest

From a letter, dated August 1856, to his Mother.

Many thanks for your love and prayers which have been abundantly answered, and in the midst of trial the love of God has abundantly been revealed, supporting and – I do not say comforting merely – but causing me to rejoice in His wisdom, grace, power and love, far, far more than your weak faith had led you to expect. Oh yes! Only let the Lord reveal His love, and sorrowing we rejoice, tried we are comforted, perplexed we are not cast down, bereaved we do not despair.

I cannot say, as Lady Maxwell did, 'He shall have my whole heart', for I feel so helpless and powerless, I cannot withhold from earthly affection and cleavings to the dust; but I can and do pray, 'Take it, Lord, take it, and keep it to the day of Thine appearing.'

[After a long account of having been robbed of all, he continues] I sometimes wonder if I shall ever be settled, and long for a fixed and permanent position and a partner to share in all my joys and sorrows, labours and encouragements. But the only true rest is in following Jesus whithersoever He goes; the only true repose is in labouring for Him. And while I long for quiet, even now, after a week of it, I long to be at work again, speaking of Jesus' love.

At home you can never know what it is to be alone – absolutely alone, without one friend, with everyone looking on you with curiosity, with contempt, with suspicion or with dislike. Thus to learn what it is to be despised and rejected of men, thus to learn what it is to have nowhere to lay your head, and then to have the love of Jesus applied to your heart by the Holy Spirit – His holy, self-denying love – this is worth coming for. Oh! to know more of Him, and the power of His resurrection, and the fellowship of His sufferings, being made conformable unto His death. The flesh would say, 'Use not this prayer, you know not what you ask;' – but 'God is love'.

22nd Day

I Will Talk of Thy Doings.

From a letter to his sister Amelia, dated September, 1856.

'O magnify the Lord with me, and let us exalt His name together', were the words of the Psalmist of old, and are now the experience of His people. He has told us not to forsake the assembling of ourselves together, but to exhort one another. Christians need fellowship. In olden times 'they who feared the Lord spake often one to another'; and one reason why, in comparatively few years, the Methodist family has reached the position it holds at home and abroad, is no doubt the carrying out of this principle. We not only need to feel Jesus precious, but we need to speak of His inestimable worth; not only to experience His love, but to speak of His dealings. And so in trial we need to bear each other's burdens. It is as necessary to ministers as to people, to missionaries as to those at home, and yet how difficult it is to obtain.

I have been thinking a little today on that passage which exhorts us to be 'followers of God as dear children, and walk in love, as Christ also hath loved us, and hath given Himself for us, for a sweet-smelling savour'. How much is taught here! If we are to follow Him, how can we but forgive the offences of others; and resist not evil, but with unselfish, self-sacrificing love seek to promote the welfare of all, even our enemies? Jesus left the fullness of His power and glory, honour and dominion, joy and riches, for us; what can we withhold, that we seek not the well-being of the heathen, and the good of our fellow Christians?

How can so many Christians feel satisfied with giving their subscriptions to missions when they ought to give themselves? Satan surely has some subtle but powerful way of hindering. Oh! that we could all realize the Lord as our present portion, not merely future, but also present; then I think many would give themselves to the work of evangelising the heathen. May the Lord bless you, enable you to serve Him, and be a burning and a shining light.

To a Father unwilling to give up his daughter.

I would not wish you to think me so selfish and unfeeling as to suppose I have no thought of, or care for, the pain of mind you must suffer. I know the anguish you will experience in parting with one so much loved. The anxieties, the fears for her safety, which you must endure are vividly before my mind. And yet, you will not, you cannot, deny her to Him who spared not his only begotten Son. Is she your fairest, your choicest treasure? Then rejoice to have such an one to lay on the altar, to present to the Lord. Will He accept the maimed or blemished? No! He must have the firstlings of the flock, the pure and spotless – such and such only will He accept.

You are not called to *slay* your Isaac, but to present your Samuel to the Lord; and I doubt not that, remembering we are but stewards, you will be found faithful. We are called to be followers of God. He cheerfully gave His Son for the life of the world. We are told that those who love Jesus will keep His commandments, and He says, 'Go ye out into all the world and preach the Gospel to every creature.' You will not prevent your daughter serving Him who has called her by His grace. True it is that her course will not, perhaps, be one appreciated by the world. No earthly coronet will adorn her brow, nor pomp, nor state attend her steps. But how much more honourable to be the Ambassador to the only true Potentate, to the King of kings and Lord of lords. And hereafter, a crown of glory that fadeth not away.

'Shall we, whose souls are lighted with wisdom from on high, Shall we, to souls benighted, the lamp of light deny?' Or rather let me say: 'Can we?' If so, it is time to examine ourselves, whether we are still in the gall of bitterness or not.... We want those who feel the value of their own souls; who are able to appreciate the awful fate they themselves have escaped, and who realize the joy of the glorious inheritance in store for them; and who can form some conception of the position of those in this benighted land.

Human and Divine Love

To his sister Amelia on her betrothal.

I hope you are making the use, and gaining the spiritual benefits from your engagement which you may do and ought to do. These feelings are planted in the heart by God, and all the circumstances connected with them are ordained or allowed by Him for our highest spiritual good, as well as temporal happiness; and in so far as we make that use of them we may expect blessing to attend them. They are used by the Holy Spirit to typify the love and relationship between God and His people in nearly every, if not every, book in the Bible.

With that love you love your husband (in fact or anticipation), you are to love Jesus – nay, more. Are you sad and lonely when he leaves you? So you should be when Jesus is absent. Do you long for the completion of your union? So you should for the return of Jesus to take you to Himself. Is service for him freedom? No, you will say, that is far too cold a term. Freedom! It is joy, pleasure, the desire of my heart. So you should serve Jesus. Would you do what you could to remove the obstacles and hasten your union? Then look for and hasten the day of His return. See Jesus in everything, then in everything you will find blessing.

Look to Jesus! Do nothing but for Him, but as in Him and by Him (*i.e.* by His strength and direction). Christ all and in all. And oh! may He abundantly and personally manifest Himself to you. You will think I am writing you a long lecture on this topic; but I am sure the happiness of your union will very much depend upon your realization and practising of these things. He must love you as Christ loved the Church, and you must love, honour and obey Christ, or you will not get the blessing God intends you from it. And another thought: Whatsoever you do, do all to the glory of God. Seek His glory, do His will, and this shall be added to you. There is no prayer so frequently and practically useful as: 'Not my will but Thine be done.'

God's Plans Go Forward

From a letter to his Mother, dated April, 1857.

This is one of China's crises: very soon it may be open, very soon it may be closed. We must work as we have opportunity; and should we be stopped for a time by the providence of God, we know He can make seed already sown to spring without the sower's instrumentality. His plans ever go forward, though to us they may appear at times retrograde – that is from our imperfection. May we ever grow in grace, be made such vessels as our Master can use, and soon we shall have an entrance given us into the everlasting Kingdom of our God and Saviour.

We have our portion; 'our Beloved is ours, and we are His'. 'He is fairer than the sons of men', without spot or blemish. 'His name is like ointment poured forth.' May we see more of Him; may we daily see more in Him! Looking to Him, even through a glass darkly, may we be growing in likeness to Him, longing to be with Him, longing to be like Him. Like Him freed from sin, like Him pure and holy, like Him well-pleasing to God, like Him freed from sorrow, pain and tears. 'We shall be satisfied when we awake with His likeness;' 'in His presence there is fullness of joy, at His right hand there are pleasures for evermore.'

I have been much tired of late. Seeking to do all to the glory of God, I do nothing not mixed with self and sin. Oh! how fit is our Jesus for us; perfect righteousness for ruined sinners; a glorious robe for the tattered and filthy; gold, fine gold, for the poor; sight for the blind – all we need, all we could wish. Precious Jesus, may we love Thee more, and more manifest our love by deadness to the world. Soon we shall love with purer, stronger love, and rejoice that we were counted worthy to tread in the footsteps of our Forerunner, who is now entered for us within the veil, and ever pleads the sacrifice He once offered for our sins.

26th Day

On Seeking Guidance

To his future Brother-in-law, B. B. under date April 1857.

I am sorry in some respects that your mind is still unsettled as to offering yourself for foreign work, but in others I am glad. That it is so long and so strongly impressed on your mind is in itself an indication of some kind.

I do not think we do well to appoint times when we will decide; we had better wait on the Lord, wait His time, be it long or short, and He will show us what to do when He sees the time is come. Expect not to see your way always open before you, if you would walk by faith. When the Israelites were in the wilderness, they were led by God. They knew not when the cloud would arise and be the signal for them to move, whether it would be by day or by night. When they saw it arise they knew not in what direction, nor how far it would go. Read the account in Numbers 9. So with us if we are led by God. To the eye of unbelief we shall at times seem to be losing time; at others, seem to be going backwards, it may be. But it is the Lord's way and will end in the promised land.

If, with a simple desire to know His will and with a sincere heart, we wait on Him with earnest prayer, seeking His guidance, we shall not wait in vain; and this exercise of mind and of faith, trying, most trying to the flesh, will prove a more efficient training than all the courses of theological instruction men can devise. Keep looking to Jesus, receiving of His fullness, drinking in His teachings, seeking to tread in His footsteps, and light, joy and liberty will be yours.

If after earnest and continued prayer the foreign work is still resting on your mind, do not seek to throw it off. And may I add it? – for once these reasons had a great weight on my mind, and were a great burden to me – if the state of the Societies or religious bodies is a difficulty or hindrance, do not press your conscience or strain it; do not let pecuniary matters affect you either one way or another. The Lord will provide. His Word says so, and my experience and that of many others, proves it is so.

To his future Brother-in-law, under date April 1857.

I will write in confidence and mention things I could not otherwise do. I came out here with a stated salary. It proved insufficient, and for a time I was in a most trying and painful position.... But the Lord sent help in another way.

Since then the Society has not been able to supply me with anything approaching what I need, but through other and various channels I have not only been supplied, but have been able to help others in need, and mission work in need to a considerable extent – altogether to more than £100 during the year, quite apart from my own private and mission expenses. I do not say this in any spirit of boasting, but to show you it is no vain thing to trust in the Lord. If we glory, let us glory in Him.

I should add that this year my own expenses have not been inconsiderable – when I was robbed I lost things to the value of more than £50, and much of this had to be replaced. The Lord supplies money when it is needed, and, as you well know, there are some times when from circumstances altogether beyond our control a month's expenses are greater than three at other times. Now our Father knows our needs, and hears the cry of His people. I do not wish to urge you to come out without being connected with any Society, or without a salary; but if you cannot get these, and still are called to come, rejoice at the liberty you will thus have, and trust your Father's love. Unless you had this confidence in Him which would enable you, if called, to do so, you would find much trial here; for the nature of the work is such, if carried on in the interior, that it takes one away from those protections the flesh leans on.

I feel much condemned at my want of zeal, and coldness of heart. Oh! it will be a happy day when Jesus presents His unveiled beauties to our unclouded vision. Oh! to be kept looking by faith, even now, to our precious Jesus. Oh! to be able to receive His words, and not men's explaining of them away to nothing.

From a letter to his sister Amelia, dated May 1857.

I wish that I could have half-an-hour's conversation with you tonight. How much there is I could tell you, and hear from you. I do so long for someone with whom to have unrestricted communion, but my Father has seen it best to deny this at present, and with thankfulness I would own His love in the painful dispensations of His providence at which the flesh rebels. Faith, the evidence of things not seen, gives us victory over the world, and enables us to rejoice in being counted worthy to be followers of Him who, though the Son, 'was made perfect through suffering'.

Though we seem to be tried sometimes almost beyond our powers, we never find Him unable or unwilling to aid and sustain us; and were our hearts attuned to entire submission to His will, and did we desire it only to be done, how much fewer and lighter would our afflictions seem.

I have been very much tired of late, but the principle cause I find to be want of entire submission and passive lying in the hands of God, my strength. Oh! to desire His will to be done with my whole heart, to seek His glory with a single eye, to realize more of the fulness of our precious Jesus; to live more in the light of His countenance; to be satisfied with what He bestows; to be grateful for the favours He confers; to be ever looking to Him, treading in His steps, and waiting His speedy return.

Why do we love Him so little? It is not that He is not lovely. He is 'fairer than the children of men', 'the altogether lovely'. It is not that He does not love us; that He showed on Calvary. Oh! to be hourly, momentarily longing, hungering, thirsting for His presence. Pray that God may supply all my need, that Jesus may be all my delight, His service all my desire, and rest with Him all my hope.

A Glimpse of His Glory

Letter written amidst much peril, 4 a.m.,
October 19, 1854, to his sister Amelia.

There is something sublime in contemplating the majesty of God; His wisdom, His power, His omnipresence, too, are themes *we* love to dwell on – and why? Because we have caught a glimpse – faint it may be and is – but we *have* caught a glimpse of the *brightness of His glory*, have been shewn the express image of His person in the face of Jesus Christ, and have learned at Calvary, that *God is love. This* is the reason we now love to dwell on His other attributes, because they are *our Father's* attributes; this is the thought that makes our poor ice-bound hearts glow and burn again; this is the thought that can unseal the fountain of our tears, and melt us into adoring love and gratitude. Oh! that it were ever in our hearts, ever in our mouths. Oh! that it formed the theme of our every conversation and were never, even for a moment, lost sight of, over-balanced, covered up! Shall we deny *this* knowledge to the heathen! Shall we refuse to proclaim this glorious truth in the sight of the people? God forbid! May the time soon come when this rebel heart shall be baptised with holy fire, and this mouth shall be able intelligibly to utter the overflowing feelings of a heart wholly devoted to the service of 'Him who hath loved us'.

The Prayer of David

Blessed be the Lord God, the God of Israel, who only doeth
wondrous things. And blessed be His glorious name for ever:
and let the whole earth be filled with His glory; Amen and Amen
(Psalm 72:18, 19).

This prayer is still the prayer of the Church of the living God.
We bless His glorious name for the wondrous openings and
blessings He is giving us; but this prayer is still unfulfilled, and
will be while the Gospel of the kingdom remains unpreached for
a witness to any nation – nay, while any *one* of the 'other sheep',
whom the Father has given to His Son, has not heard His voice and
been brought from the dark mountains of sin, and safely folded,
to the joy of the Good Shepherd and of those who love Him.

In the meantime He is working ('My Father worketh hitherto,
and I work') and *He* 'will not be in rest until He have finished the
thing', and has presented to Himself His perfected Bride. The
Good Shepherd – in the person of His members – is going after
each sheep that is lost *until He find it.* How can He rest while
one of His flock is wandering in the kingdom of darkness? 'My
head is filled with dew, and My locks with the drops of the night.'
Shall we not seek deeper fellowship with Him in this blessed
work of rescuing the perishing?

A Prayer of Hudson Taylor

Found in a letter dated Ningpo, July 9, 1858.

Blessed Jesus, who did'st with Thine own heart's blood redeem each one of Thy members, wilt Thou not with more of Thine own Spirit baptize Thy people, that this people, perishing for lack of knowledge, may also be fed with living manna, and have the light of life!